AF597999

Biography in Early Modern France 1540–1630
Forms and Functions

LEGENDA

LEGENDA, founded in 1995 by the European Humanities Research Centre of the University of Oxford, is now a joint imprint of the Modern Humanities Research Association and Maney Publishing. Titles range from medieval texts to contemporary cinema and form a widely comparative view of the modern humanities, including works on Arabic, Catalan, English, French, German, Greek, Italian, Portuguese, Russian, Spanish, and Yiddish literature. An Editorial Board of distinguished academic specialists works in collaboration with leading scholarly bodies such as the Society for French Studies and the British Comparative Literature Association.

MHRA

The Modern Humanities Research Association (MHRA) encourages and promotes advanced study and research in the field of the modern humanities, especially modern European languages and literature, including English, and also cinema. It also aims to break down the barriers between scholars working in different disciplines and to maintain the unity of humanistic scholarship in the face of increasing specialization. The Association fulfils this purpose primarily through the publication of journals, bibliographies, monographs and other aids to research.

Maney Publishing is one of the few remaining independent British academic publishers. Founded in 1900 the company has offices both in the UK, in Leeds and London, and in North America, in Boston. Since 1945 Maney Publishing has worked closely with learned societies, their editors, authors, and members, in publishing academic books and journals to the highest traditional standards of materials and production.

RESEARCH MONOGRAPHS IN FRENCH STUDIES

The Research Monographs in French Studies (RMFS) form a separate series within the Legenda programme and are published in association with the Society for French Studies. Individual members of the Society are entitled to purchase all RMFS titles at a discount.

The series seeks to publish the best new work in all areas of the literature, thought, theory, culture, film and language of the French-speaking world. Its distinctiveness lies in the relative brevity of its publications (40,000–50,000 words). As innovation is a priority of the series, volumes should predominantly consist of new material, although, subject to appropriate modification, previously published research may form up to one third of the whole. Proposals may include critical editions as well as critical studies. They should be sent with one or two sample chapters for consideration to Dr Ann Jefferson, New College, Oxford OX1 3BN.

PUBLISHED IN THIS SERIES

1. *Privileged Anonymity: The Writings of Madame de Lafayette* by Anne Green
2. *Stéphane Mallarmé. Correspondance: compléments et suppléments* edited by Lloyd James Austin, Bertrand Marchal and Nicola Luckhurst
3. *Critical Fictions: Nerval's 'Les Illuminés'* by Meryl Tyers
4. *Towards a Cultural Philology* by Amy Wygant
5. *George Sand and Autobiography* by Janet Hiddleston
6. *Expressivism* by Johnnie Gratton
7. *Memory and Survival: The French Cinema of Krzysztof Kieślowski* by Emma Wilson
8. *Between Sequence and 'Sirventes'* by Catherine Léglu
9. *All Puns Intended* by Walter Redfern
10. *Saint-Evremond: A Voice From Exile* edited by Denys Potts
11. *La Cort d'Amor: A Critical Edition* edited by Matthew Bardell
12. *Race and the Unconscious* by Celia Britton
13. *Proust: La Traduction du sensible* by Nathalie Aubert
14. *Silent Witness: Racine's Non-Verbal Annotations of Euripides* by Susanna Phillippo
15. *Robert Antelme: Humanity, Community, Testimony* by Martin Crowley
16. *By the People for the People?: Eugène Sue's 'Les Mystères de Paris'* by Christopher Prendergast
17. *Alter Ego: The Critical Writings of Michel Leiris* by Seán Hand
18. *Two Old French Satires on the Power of the Keys* edited by Daron Burrows
19. *Oral Narration in Modern French: A Linguistic Analysis of Temporal Patterns* by Janice Carruthers
20. *Selfless Cinema? Ethics and French Documentary* by Sarah Cooper
21. *Poisoned Words: Slander and Satire in Early Modern France* by Emily Butterworth
22. *France/China: Intercultural Imaginings* by Alex Hughes
23. *Biography in Early Modern France 1540–1630: Forms and Functions* by Katherine MacDonald
24. *Balzac and the Model of Painting* by Diana Knight

www.rmfs.mhra.org.uk

Biography in Early Modern France 1540–1630

Forms and Functions

Katherine MacDonald

Research Monographs in French Studies 23
Modern Humanities Research Association and Maney Publishing
2007

Published in association with the Society for French Studies by the Modern Humanities Research Association and Maney Publishing
1 Carlton House Terrace
London SW1Y 5DB
United Kingdom

LEGENDA is an imprint of the Modern Humanities Research Association and Maney Publishing

Maney Publishing is the trading name of W. S. Maney & Son Ltd, whose registered office is at Suite 1C, Joseph's Well, Hanover Walk, Leeds LS3 1AB

ISBN 978-1-905981-11-3

First published 2007

Printed in Great Britain

Cover: 875 Design

Copy-Editor: Richard Correll

CONTENTS

To My Parents

ACKNOWLEDGEMENTS

As this book is a distant cousin of a D.Phil. thesis, I would like to thank first of all my supervisor, Richard Cooper, for his unfailing support and enthusiastic encouragement at every stage of this project. I would also like to thank my two examiners, Terence Cave and John O'Brien, for their help and generous advice, especially when I came to reformulate my original topic. Many thanks to Azzedine Haddour, Kees Meerhoff and Peter Sharratt who read parts of this book, shared their own work and made perceptive comments. I am grateful to Jann Matlock, with whom I discussed this project at length, and whose acute remarks and suggestions proved invaluable. Una Roman D'Elia provided expert advice on the choice of artwork for the cover. Thanks also are due to my two readers at Legenda, for their extremely helpful comments. I am especially grateful to Ann Jefferson, the editor of this series, for her encouragement and her thoughtful and careful reading, and to Graham Nelson at Legenda for his generous help and support. I would like to thank the Arts and Humanities Research Council and the Department of French, University College London, for funding a year's research leave which made timely completion of this project possible.

INTRODUCTION

> Les escrits de Plutarque, à les bien savourer, nous le descouvrent assez, et je pense le connoistre jusques dans l'ame; si voudrois-je que nous eussions quelques memoires de sa vie; et me suis jetté en ce discours à quartier à propos du bon gré que je sens à Aulus Gellius de nous avoir laissé par escrit ce conte de ses meurs qui revient à mon suject de la cholere.
>
> MONTAIGNE, *Essais*, II, 31 [1580]

This book takes its starting point from Montaigne's statement of interest in the life of his favourite biographer, Plutarch. Although, as a careful reader, Montaigne believed that he could see through Plutarch's writings into his very soul, he still desired some formal account of the sage from Chaironea. Furthermore, Montaigne wished such 'memoires' of Plutarch's life to come from a fellow ancient writer, someone who belonged to the same cultural world. In the absence of any surviving ancient *Life* of Plutarch, Montaigne was grateful for the fragmentary anecdote about Plutarch's moral conduct transmitted by Aulus Gellius. Plutarch's Renaissance editors evidently considered that other readers might share Montaigne's curiosity about the biographer's life. At the end of the sixteenth century, a life of Plutarch by Xylander appeared in a Latin edition of his complete works (both *Lives* and *Moral Essays*).[1]

Admittedly, in the above quotation Montaigne did not distinguish between Plutarch as the author of the *Moral Essays*, and Plutarch the biographer. Still, Montaigne's curiosity about the career of a writer whose fame rested significantly on his treatment of the lives of others does prompt some intriguing questions about the production of biography in sixteenth-century France.

Biography in any period lends itself to study from a variety of angles. One obvious reason for the diversity of possible critical treatments is that any act of biography implicates at least three distinct figures: the person about whom the biography was written (the 'subject' or protagonist), the biographer, and the reader.

Montaigne's remarks aside, most Renaissance discussions of biography tended to concentrate on either the reader or the subject, and ignore the biographer. Renaissance theoreticians of biography were keenly interested in how it might perpetuate the fame of the great men who were its subjects. The reader was equally important, though, because of a widely held view, inherited from Plutarch, of *Lives* as providing examples of virtue to imitate or vice to avoid.[2] Thus, in a mid-1570s discussion of biography, a Florentine learned society, the Accademia degli Alterati, associated it with the handbook of statecraft or manual of morals.[3] Parallel to this discussion, the academicians embarked on a programme of reading of Plutarch's

Lives which they hoped might stimulate new production of biography in the same normative vein. In 1550s France, translators of ancient biography, like Georges de la Boutière, who produced a version of Suetonius's *Lives of the Twelve Caesars*, or Jacques Amyot, translator of Plutarch, insisted in their prefaces on how such works could edify readers and even transform them in the image of the subject.

Renaissance writers did not completely overlook the agency of the biographer, though. Francis Bacon, in *The Advancement of Learning* (1605), articulated the traditional conception of *Lives* as works endowed with the potential to guarantee the posthumous fame of their subjects. Still, lamenting the dearth of such writing in his day, Bacon proceeded to suggest the importance of the figure of the biographer, alongside that of the subject. In his discussion of biography, Bacon related Ludovico Ariosto's picturesque version of the myth of the three Fates.[4] According to Ariosto's mythology, at the end of the thread of every man's life lay a medal containing his name. When death cut this thread, Time caught the medal as it fell and took it to Lethe, the river of oblivion. There, many birds flying around might snatch the medal and carry it a little distance before dropping it once more. Only if a swan happened to get the medal in its beak did the name travel as far as a temple, presumably that of Fame, where it might be consecrated. Thus, Bacon's allegorical account of biography, in addition to insisting on the cult of great men, does incidentally attract some attention on to the figure of the biographer — the exceptional swan who had the strength and dedication of purpose to carry the medal as far as the temple.

This book, then, attempts to interpret the behaviour of Bacon's swans. It premises that, if we are to understand the forms and functions of biography in the early modern period, we must be alert to its social and cultural contexts and, in particular, to the figure of the biographer himself. I shall be investigating the ways in which biography, by supporting the biographer's identification with his subject, provided a vehicle for the advancement of the biographer's own career. As a working hypothesis I contend that a biographer's ability to recreate his subject in the text served as an advertisement, and a guarantee of his unique suitability to follow in the footsteps of his model outside the confines of the text. In terms of cultural history, then, my study of biography seeks to contribute a new understanding of this form of writing as a means of self-promotion. In so doing, I hope it may generate valuable insights into the modes and dynamics of courtly patronage.

Up until the latter part of the twentieth century, the critical approach to early modern biography most commonly encountered amongst scholars of the period has been one which engaged primarily with the protagonist. Those who studied biography in this way generally considered it as evidence for the reputation and fortune of the great personalities of the era. The frequency of this approach shows a tendency to lionize yet further the outstanding geniuses about whom *Lives* were written, rather than to pay any heed to the minor authors who piously chronicled their existence. As a consequence of such a critical modus operandi, these biographies received little study on their own terms. Historians and literary scholars concentrated almost exclusively on what such texts revealed about their individual protagonists' lives, and did not generally attend to the circumstances of their production or to their place within the career of the biographer, who remained a shadowy figure.

As evidence of this critical tendency one need only adduce that although the subjects of the biographies examined in this book were and are important, their biographers have not themselves become well known, even to specialists of the period. Guillaume Budé (1467–1540), one of France's great humanists, vastly overshadows his biographer and junior colleague, Louis Le Roy (1510?–77). Guy du Faur de Pibrac (1529–84), whose *Quatrains* were, as Jean Lafond noted, 'le traité de morale pratique le plus souvent édité, le plus répandu en France, et hors de France même, jusqu'au milieu du XVIIe siècle',[5] remains relatively much better known than Charles Paschal (1547–1625). The posthumous reputation of Pierre de Ronsard (1524–85) almost completely obscures that of the minor poet Claude Binet (1533?–1600). The renown of Pierre de la Ramée (or Ramus, 1515–72), one of the most original thinkers of the century, towers over that of his former pupil and biographer Nicolas de Nancel (1539–1610). The one autobiography I discuss is by one of the major poets of the century, Agrippa d'Aubigné (1552–1630).

In more recent years however, scholars, most particularly in the field of English Renaissance studies, have begun to take an interest in the figure of the early modern biographer as a creative writer. This critical turn is largely the consequence of a trend amongst late twentieth-century scholarly biographers themselves to focus on the self-presentation or self-fashioning of their early modern subjects. Thus Stephen Greenblatt, in his treatment of the life of Sir Walter Ralegh, Mario Biagioli, in his account of Galileo and Lisa Jardine, in her analysis of Erasmus's textual self-construction, considered their protagonists' concern with self-advancement and self-promotion and their efforts to conform to the codes of European court culture.[6] One notable example of a scholar whose discussion of early modern biography makes use of Greenblatt's work on self-fashioning is Judith Anderson, who explores the relationship between truth and fiction in Tudor–Stuart biography.[7] Anderson charts the emergence of an awareness of fiction in early modern biography and of the biographer's growing consciousness of his power to form and even contrive the human image. Working along related lines, Kevin Pask has examined the role of early modern biographers in constructing early modern identity in England. Pask's study of early *Lives* of poets such as Philip Sidney, Edmund Spenser and John Donne traces the emergence of the English author.[8] In a similar vein, students of early modern autobiography are now finely attuned to culturally determined rules for self-presentation, to the tendency to perceive the self in terms of certain roles, and to the ways in which autobiographers have scripted their lives in terms of certain plots — for example, conversion narratives.[9]

Both the creative role of the biographer and the social function of biography emerge vividly from the work of Claude-Gilbert Dubois. In an article surveying forms of biography in Europe from 1560 to 1600, Dubois has evoked the sociological conditions in which biographers produced their works. As a rule, early modern biographers composed monograph *Lives* of individuals in two sets of circumstances. First, a biographer might receive a commission from a powerful family who sought to bask in the reflected glory of an illustrious ancestor. Second, he might write a *Life* in homage to a potential patron who had some association with its subject, such as a bond of friendship, or even a shared name.[10] Re-placing biography within its social context, Dubois further observes that these works participated in the elaboration of local or familial mythologies, as well as proselytizing, in the case of minority groups which needed to establish themselves.[11] He concludes that the biographer's purpose in composing his text shaped its symbolic meaning. Since this symbolic dimension generally took precedence over fidelity to the truth, the correct interpretation of works of biography necessitates an awareness of the biographer and his aims.

All of the scholars mentioned thus far foreground the active role of early modern biographers in shaping the identity of their protagonists. To a considerable extent, this approach necessarily remains primarily engaged with the subjects of biography. This is especially the case since the biographers were often continuing a programme of self-fabrication or construction of identity initiated by the subject himself. My study, whilst informed by the work of these scholars, shifts its focus on to the ways in which biography assisted early modern biographers in the construction of their own identity. Thus, early modern biography, when viewed in its cultural and social contexts, emerges not only as an act of textual representation or construction of identity of the protagonist, but also as a projection of the future self of the biographer.

My view of biography as integral to the self-formation of the biographer relates closely to Timothy Hampton's discussion of exemplarity and its representation in the late Renaissance.[12] Hampton posits that 'the representation of the exemplary figure functions as the occasion for reflection on the constitution of the self'.[13] The heroic or virtuous figure offers an icon of excellence after which the reader is to be formed. Hampton further notes the crucial role of biographical narrative in this process of self-transformation and draws a parallel with psychoanalysis. In psychoanalysis, making sense of one's present life entails appropriating one's past, through a process of writing or composing one's own life narrative. Humanist exemplarity, by comparison, advocates applying the narrative of someone else's life to one's present situation.[14] I am interested in how, for the biographer, the creative work of fashioning the life narrative of exemplary figure necessarily becomes intertwined with self-presentation.

My approach to biography also has implications for its generic classification, since by using the life narratives of their subjects to pre-script (or recast) their own careers, early modern biographers effectively blurred the boundaries between biography and autobiography. The gap between the two further narrows when we consider the production of biography as an act of creative reception. The biographer's transformation of lived-life into a written *Life* was a process which often involved 'bricolage' as the biographer included autobiographical fragments gleaned from the subject's own writings in the form of letters, draft memoirs, or first-person statements contained in his other works.

This book, then, presents case studies of four exemplary biographies and one autobiography of major intellectual figures spanning the period 1540–1630. I have chosen to restrict my study to biographies of men of letters by their fellow men of letters, for two reasons. First, the monograph life of the French writer was a notable innovation of this period, which, authorized by Italian biographies of

Petrarch, Boccaccio and Dante, took its place alongside the more established forms of royal biography, hagiography, and biographical encyclopaedia. Over the course of the sixteenth century in France, writers self-consciously re-adapted ancient and medieval forms of biography, and from the 1520s biography evolved into a remarkably protean and fertile mode of writing. The same impulse which led sixteenth-century editors to insert a *Life* of Plutarch in Xylander's 1599 edition of his complete works also prompted them to include many other author-biographies in contemporary editions. Not only ancient writers, such as Plutarch and Seneca, or Homer and Virgil, but near contemporaries Dante, Petrarch and Boccaccio, as well as authors of the day, like Erasmus and Budé, or the poets Ariosto and Ronsard, all received literary commemoration in this fashion.[15] On the one hand, editors may simply have been responding to the contemporary appetite for biography. The rediscovery of ancient biography which began with the *Lives* of emperors and generals by Plutarch, Suetonius and Cornelius Nepos soon extended to biographies of philosophers, sophists and grammarians by Diogenes Laërtius, Suetonius and Philostratus. On the other hand, the addition of the last three to the biographical canon reflects the growing contemporary interest in the lives of *personæ privatæ* (writers, philosophers, artists) and not just *personæ publicæ* (emperors, generals, etc).[16]

My second reason for limiting my study to biographies of men of letters is that I am especially interested in the ways in which these texts promoted collective identity in a particular socio-cultural group. This group roughly corresponds to that of George Huppert's *bourgeois gentilshommes*: neither clearly 'noble' in the established, military sense of the word (*noblesse de race* or *d'épée*), nor belonging to the merchant bourgeoisie (*roturiers*).[17] Their social ascent during this period of French history has been described by Huppert and, more recently, by Gilbert Gadoffre, as a kind of 'cultural revolution'.[18] An emergent elite, the *bourgeois gentilshommes* sought to cement their new status through the acquisition of cultural as well as material capital. In addition to the purchase of offices in the royal administration, they relied upon accomplishments in the field of *bonæ litteræ* ('good letters') to gain them positions of influence in government and thus to secure 'noble' identity. As biographer, the humanist man of letters situated himself within the same cultural field as his subject, thereby accrediting himself as a fellow man of letters by his own display of humanistic competence.

Early modern biographers inscribed themselves in the biographies they wrote of their fellow men of letters in manifold ways which supported the formation of this group identity. My approach to biography thus draws on a variety of cultural material to illuminate these *Lives*. Biographers of men of letters responded to the social demands of the newly emerging magisterial class, as well as to escalating religious and political tensions, with a vigorously developing rhetoric. This rhetoric was enriched by contact with multiple literary genres (e.g., drama, narrative fiction) and other non-literary discourses (e.g., treatises on civility and diplomacy containing portraits of the ideal courtier or ambassador; political pamphlets; letters; 'scientific' works on physiognomy and medicine which purport to describe the intellectual, or man of genius). Nevertheless, my study, whilst broadly informed by new historicist criticism, remains grounded in literary close reading and historical analysis.

This book includes five case studies chosen to reveal the diverse ways in which biographies of men of letters operated as negotiations in the world. Each chapter develops a major theme in relation to a case which contributes to our understanding of biography's cultural function: (1) the relationship between biographical narrative and humanist historiography; (2) the intersection between biography, courtiership and diplomacy; (3) the early modern conception of poetry; (4) the application to biography of learned and practical medical expertise; and (5) the notion of the court as a theatre.

Chapter 1, then, analyses the biography of Budé by the promising young Hellenist, Le Roy. I argue that Le Roy's *Vita Budæi* acted as a conduit for the expression of the biographer's professional ambitions. At the same time, this pragmatic function of biography shaped the contours of Le Roy's narrative of Budé's life. Le Roy's desire to forge a reputation for himself as a scholar by announcing his philosophy of history influenced the form of the plot he employed in recounting Budé's life. I identify a similar scenario in Chapter 2, on the *Life* of Pibrac by Paschal. Like Le Roy, Paschal was also a young courtier who needed to assure the progression of his career within the royal administration. Paschal chose to highlight Pibrac's diplomatic career as a way of attracting attention to his own ambitions and talents in this field. Chapter 3, on the *Vie de Ronsard*, tests my central thesis in that it marks the end of the biographer Binet's poetic career at the same time as it consecrates the entry of its protagonist into literary history. Chapter 4 treats Nancel's *P. Rami Vita*. Despite being composed later in its author's life, the *Vita* (published 1599, although Nancel began writing it some twenty years earlier) still manifests a preoccupation with imitation as a vehicle for social and cultural insertion. Nancel published the *Vita* at a distance of over twenty years from the death of his teacher, Ramus. Although Nancel enjoyed a lucrative medical career, he often complained of his difficulty in publishing his many scholarly manuscripts. By writing a biography of an established scholar, Nancel advertised his ability to imitate his master and sought entry into the scholarly community. Finally, Chapter 5 discusses the only autobiography under consideration, and the only text by a Protestant. D'Aubigné's *Sa Vie à ses enfants* nonetheless more closely resembles the other life narratives discussed than the modern segregation of biography and autobiography would imply. Like the preceding examples of biography, *Sa Vie* mediates between individual and collectivity by providing a mechanism whereby the younger generation might fit itself into the existing cultural framework, despite social instability and religious persecution. I shall argue that, in addition to moral instruction, d'Aubigné's autobiography imparted to his children by example the courtly survival skills of play-acting and stage-managing. At the heart of *Sa Vie* thus lies an intriguing paradox: that someone in perpetual conflict with his milieu participated in the theatricality which characterized the courts of Henri III and Henri de Navarre. Chapter 5 shows how theatrical elements such as costume, gesture, stage-business and props, and internal audience served as key narrative devices in *Sa Vie à ses enfants*.

Notes to the Introduction

1. *Plutarchi quæ extant omnia cum latina interpretatione H. Cruserii, G. Xylandri et doctorum virorum notis*, 2 vols (Frankfurt: A. Wecheli heredes, C. Marnium and J. Aubrium, 1599). Xylander cobbled together his biography of Plutarch fairly uncritically from numerous first-person statements scattered throughout his works. At least one edition of Amyot's version of the *Lives* also featured a French translation of Xylander's biography of Plutarch: *Les Vies des hommes illustres grecs et romains*, 9 vols (Geneva: J. Stoer, 1604–10).
2. See, for example Plutarch's preface to his 'Pericles', in *The Rise and Fall of Athens*, trans. by Ian Scott-Kilvert (Harmondsworth: Penguin, 1960), pp. 165–66.
3. Vanni Bramanti, 'Introduzione' in Torquato Malaspina, *Dello scrivere le vite*, ed. by Vanni Bramanti (Bergamo: Moretti & Vitali, 1991), p. 12.
4. Francis Bacon, 'The Advancement of Learning', in *The Major Works*, ed. by Brian Vickers (Oxford: Oxford University Press, 2002), pp. 120–299 (p. 182).
5. Jean Lafond, *Moralistes du XVII siècle* (Paris: R. Laffont, 1992), p. 5.
6. Stephen Greenblatt, *Sir Walter Ralegh: The Renaissance Man and his Roles* (New Haven, CT: Yale University Press, 1973); Mario Biagioli, *Galileo Courtier: The Practice of Science in the Culture of Absolutism* (Chicago: University of Chicago Press, 1993); Lisa Jardine, *Erasmus, Man of Letters: The Construction of Charisma in Print* (Princeton, NJ: Princeton University Press, 1993).
7. Judith Anderson, *Biographical Truth: The Representation of Historical Persons in Tudor–Stuart Writing* (New Haven, CT: Yale University Press, 1984), p. 7.
8. Kevin Pask, *The Emergence of the English Author: Pre-Scripting the Life of the Poet in Early Modern England* (Cambridge: Cambridge University Press, 1996).
9. Peter Burke, *What is Cultural History?* (Cambridge: Polity Press, 2004), p. 88.
10. Claude-Gilbert Dubois, 'L'Individu dans la société et dans l'histoire. Formes de la biographie dans la période 1560–1600', *Nouvelle Revue du Seizième Siècle*, 19.1 (2001), 83–105 (p. 91).
11. Dubois, p. 92.
12. Timothy Hampton, *Writing from History: The Rhetoric of Exemplarity in Renaissance Literature* (Ithaca, NY: Cornell University Press, 1990). On Renaissance exemplarity, see also John Lyons, *Exemplum: The Rhetoric of Example in Early Modern France and Italy* (Princeton, NJ: Princeton University Press, 1989).
13. Hampton, p. xi.
14. Hampton, p. 22.
15. Peter Burke, 'A Invenção da Biografia e o Individualismo Renascentista', *Estudos Históricos, Rio de Janeiro*, 19 (1997), 1–14.
16. Jozef Ijsewijn, 'Die humanistische Biographie', in *Biographie und Autobiographie in der Renaissance*, ed. by August Buck (Wiesbaden: O. Harrassowitz, 1983), pp. 1–19 (p. 7).
17. George Huppert, *Les Bourgeois Gentilshommes: An Essay on the Definition of Elites in Renaissance France* (Chicago: The University of Chicago Press, 1977).
18. Gilbert Gadoffre, *La Révolution culturelle dans la France des humanistes. Guillaume Budé et François Ier* (Geneva: Droz, 1997).

Figure 1. Portrait of Budé from Jean-Jacques Boissard, *Bibliotheca chalcographica, hoc est virtute et eruditione clarorum virorum imagines* (Heidelberg: Clemens Ammon, 1669), p. 117.

CHAPTER 1

'Puis que peut faire un courtisan vagabond?' Le Roy's *Gulielmi Budæi Vita* (1540)

On 22 August 1540, Guillaume Budé (b. 1468), the great pioneer of Greek studies in France and instigator of the humanist Collège royal (the future Collège de France), died of a protracted bout of fever. According to his biographer and fellow Hellenist Louis Le Roy (1510?–1577), the physical agony Budé experienced paled in comparison to his mental horror at the prospect of his imminent death.[1] This rather unchristian attitude warrants some explanation, especially in the case of a scholar who had been preoccupied throughout his career with reconciling the secular study of the arts with his Christian vocation.[2] Le Roy duly provided clarification: Budé did not shrink from death out of a selfish excessive attachment to his own life — on the contrary, as Le Roy hoped his biography would amply demonstrate, Budé's outstanding works of scholarship guaranteed his immortal fame and his piety secured the passage of his spirit to a better place. No, Budé hesitated to depart from this world because he feared for the material well-being of his family. During his life he had elected to set his studies above the advancement of his magisterial career.[3] Now that he saw his end approaching, Budé bitterly regretted not having paid more attention to securing the family fortunes.[4]

As the father of eleven children including seven sons, Budé's concerns were, it turns out, partially justified. Although Le Roy did not see fit to mention this in the *Gulielmi Budæi Vita*, Budé had entrusted his sons' careers to the current chancellor, his own patron and friend Guillaume Poyet (1473–1548, chancellor 1538–1542).[5] This would doubtless have seemed a prudent move, for, at the time of Budé's death, Poyet stood at the height of his power. As effective prime minister of France, the chancellor's influence with the king, François I, easily eclipsed that of the other two royal officers in charge of the navy and the army respectively, the admiral Philippe de Chabot (1492–1543) and the connétable, Anne de Montmorency (1492–1567), by whose agency Poyet had been appointed.

Of the same generation as Budé's sons, the thirty-year-old Le Roy had only just returned to Paris in 1540, fresh from a stint at Toulouse's famous law faculty. Despite his recent arrival at court, Le Roy certainly knew about the current chancellor's importance in the royal administration and about Poyet's patronage of Budé. Indeed, on the advice of a local prelate, Philippe de Cossé, bishop of Le Roy's native Coutances in Normandy, he dedicated the *Vita* to Poyet as Budé's intimate friend. As he wrote in the dedication to Poyet, Le Roy hoped that the *Vita* would provide him, as yet an obscure young law student, with access to the great royal officer.[6]

Still, even an aspiring scholar with such impeccable humanistic credentials as those of Le Roy, the favoured student of Budé's disciple Jacques Toussain (1490?–1547),[7] took a calculated risk in approaching Poyet for support. Poyet's power made him often arrogant, for one thing. Moreover, contemporary opinions diverged on Poyet's susceptibility to act as a patron of letters. Some, like the orientalist and cabbalist Guillaume Postel (1510–81), consistently upheld, often against the evidence, Poyet's commitment to humanism ('bonæ literæ'/ 'good letters') and in particular to Budé's pet project, the instauration of a trilingual (Greek, Latin and Hebrew) college under royal patronage. Others upbraided Poyet for allowing fiscal concerns to impede its establishment in a palace to be built on the left bank of the Seine, directly facing the Louvre, a powerful visual symbol of the importance of the new humanism to the monarchy. While the Italian humanist, churchman and poet, Jacopo Sadoleto (1477–1547) praised Poyet's eloquence, detractors abounded.[8]

Le Roy nonetheless seems to have achieved his mercenary ends, winning a place in Poyet's household soon after penning the dedication of the *Vita*. As for Budé's heirs, the chancellor's protection served them rather less well, or perhaps they lacked the adroitness needed to turn it to their advantage. In 1541, for example, the assembly of Paris municipal magistrates, the 'Conseil des échevins' rejected Budé's son Dreux as municipal councillor because Poyet, who had more than once held Parliament in contempt, had recommended him.[9] Le Roy, though, proved a marginally more skilful operator. Despite Poyet's disgrace and imprisonment for fiscal impropriety (1542), Le Roy managed to retain his post in the chancellery. Relatively untarnished by his early association with Poyet, Le Roy remained in the employ of his successors François Errault (d. 1544, 'garde des sceaux' or minister of justice, 1543) and François Olivier (1487–1560, chancellor 1545–60).[10] Still, for the next ten years, Le Roy would follow the court as a 'courtisan vagabond', taking up commissions as they were offered — including missions involving travel to England, Germany, and Italy — but not obtaining a secure post.[11] During this period, Le Roy attempted to consolidate his reputation as a humanist by producing a series of French translations from Greek philosophers and orators.[12] Budé had made his scholarly début in similar fashion: his first publication was a Latin translation of Plutarch's *De placitis philosophorum* (*On the opinions of the philosophers*, Paris: Josse Bade, 1505), the first published original translation of Greek by any French person.[13] With the onset of the Wars of Religion in the 1560s, Le Roy turned his hand to political pamphleteering, producing a series of occasional works which demonstrate a pro-monarchist political conservatism, again in sympathy with Budé's own views.[14] Only in 1572 did Le Roy achieve a measure of security when he succeeded no less a scholar than Denis Lambin (*c.*1520–72), the renowned translator of Aristotle, as royal Professor of Greek in the humanist college Budé had lobbied so hard to found.

Thus Le Roy's career path shows a number of similarities with that of Budé.[15] A generation apart, they belonged admittedly to different social classes. The Budés owned land in the form of 'seigneuries', held important posts in royal administration and hovered on the periphery of nobility, whereas the impecunious Le Roy could claim no such pedigree. Both Le Roy and Budé, however, had received some training in law before turning to philology and in particular to Greek studies. Translation served each as a preliminary to the production of original works. Both scholars were reluctant followers of the royal court, yet staunchly defended the crown in their political writings. And the crown ultimately rewarded their monarchist, Gallican politics by conferring prestigious appointments on each man, albeit after long years of service. François I made Budé 'maître des requêtes' (literally 'master of petitions', a high-level judicial and administrative office in the royal household) in 1522, when he was sixty-four,[16] and Charles IX approved Le Roy's elevation to Royal Professor of Greek at roughly the same age.

The *Vita* may, as Kelley has observed, have 'set a formal literary seal' on Budé's reputation as France's 'arch-humanist'.[17] It also provided Le Roy with a convenient template for building his own humanistic career, a strategy we shall see the magistrate and diplomat Paschal replicate later in his *Vie de Pibrac* (Chapter 2). Le Roy's remarks about Budé's deathbed anxiety for the future prosperity of the family would thus betray his own concern with social advancement, as would his strategic choice of patron. Moreover, Le Roy's exploitation of Budé's demise by writing a memorial designed to launch his own career transcended the opportunistic solicitation of Poyet as a potential employer. The *Vita* did not just afford Le Roy the chance to bask in the reflected glory of the great Budé; even more importantly, it allowed him to introduce the philosophy of human history which would inform his mature writings. Scholars such as Gundersheimer have noted how the final pages of Le Roy's biography of Budé contain, alongside an 'entirely conventional eulogy of François I', the nucleus of his later theoretical writings about human history.[18] As Le Roy intimated in these pages of the *Vita*, universal human history possessed the dual characteristics of endless vicissitude and of cyclicality. Individual achievements in arms and letters drove a perpetual cycle of rise and fall in all civilizations. In the present happy age of renascence, both arms and letters flourished under François I. Divine providence guided the alternating cycles of rise and fall to make the underlying trajectory one of progress, and the moderns thus took precedence over the ancients. Le Roy argued passionately for their superiority on the grounds of their technological innovations, such as the printing press, gunpowder and the marine compass. He expressed this conception of history most fully in his masterwork as a mature scholar, *De la Vicissitude ou variété des choses en l'univers* (1576), a text which enjoyed considerable international success with publishers, going through five reprints in nine years and being translated into English and Italian before the end of the sixteenth century.[19]

Even in Le Roy's most distinctive work, though, he remained in the intellectual shadow of Budé. As Kelley has observed, the *Vicissitude* 'reverberates with echoes of Budé's discussion of human culture' from such philosophical works as *De studio literarum recte et commode instituendo* (*The Ways of Right Learning*, 1532), and

De philologia (*On Philology*, 1532), both of which advocated humanistic studies as enabling progress in civilization.[20] Furthermore, the *Vicissitude*, essentially a history of civilization in twelve books, has an encyclopaedic quality which places it in the direct line of Budé's own style of scholarship.[21] All of Budé's works take the same delight in displaying his immense erudition, in often unwieldy, digressive enumerations of recondite information.[22] Thus Kelley sees in the wide-ranging *Vicissitude* a popularization and continuation of Budé's thought.

In an even more immediate sense, the same applies to the earlier text of the *Vita*, for much of which the direct sources lie in Budé's published writings, in particular autobiographical passages in his correspondence with Erasmus and the English humanist Cuthbert Tunstall (1474–1559), as well as in *De philologia*.[23] Thus, by humbly transmitting to posterity his hero's own self-construction, Le Roy effectively acted as Budé's posthumous publicist, rather as Binet would later do for Ronsard (Chapter 3).[24] This description of Le Roy's working methods in compiling the *Vita* would suggest that very little of his own went into the biography. It implies that he exploited Budé's intellectual legacy for the greatest potential profit and at the least possible cost to himself: not only did he count on the biography of Budé to secure an introduction to a powerful patron, he also uncritically used Budé's autobiographical writings to compose his own text.

But Le Roy's contribution to the *Vita* does in fact make itself strongly enough felt at a different level: in the organization and patterning of the imported material as well as in the emphasis on certain themes, in particular the key theme of imitation ('imitatio'). Le Roy organized his account of Budé's life neither strictly chronologically nor thematically, employing instead a hybrid form of composition that alternated between chronological segments and thematic digressions which serve as a kind of coda to them. As I will show through close analysis of this compositional technique, Le Roy used his own conception of human history as a template for representing Budé's life in the *Vita*.

In the *Vicissitude*, Le Roy would articulate a biological developmental model for each nation which corresponded to an individual human life cycle, passing through infancy, adolescence, maturity and old age.[25] Such an anthropomorphic view of cultural history would doubtless have facilitated Le Roy's adaptation of his views of history to suit the purposes of his narration of Budé's life. But while Le Roy perceived universal history as following this pre-ordained pattern, he also conceived of it as being linear as well as cyclical, like a wave of constant frequency but increasing amplitude.[26] Periods of decline and renewal — like the present renascence of 'bonæ literæ' — alternated against a backdrop of overall progress, propelled by both divine providence, and by the actions of great men, such as Budé. Le Roy's narrative of Budé's life follows precisely the same pattern as that entailed in this view of human history. While Budé's development into France's pre-eminent Greek scholar followed an upward trajectory, a series of crises and triumphs of increasing magnitude punctuated his progress. Thus Le Roy made vicissitude into the dominant motif of his narration of Budé's life. Indeed, he structured his account around a series of crises of increasing severity which threatened Budé's status as the pre-eminent Greek scholar. Rival humanists triggered the first two of these crises when they attempted to emulate and surpass Budé, who always proved himself inimitable.

Le Roy's *Vita* traces the career of a model humanist; it therefore concentrates on his intellectual development. The first section of the biography presents Budé's beginnings as a scholar, following autobiographical segments in Budé's dialogue with François I in *De Philologia* and in his letters to fellow humanists. In adolescence Budé by his own admission wasted his time at law school at Orléans, where he failed to obtain a degree.[27] On his return to the family home, he indulged his predilection for the otiose pursuits of hunting and gambling. After this unpromising start, though, he experienced a conversion to humanism and began to study Greek.[28] This initial section of the biography concludes with an episode I shall examine in further detail later, in which two up-and-coming younger scholars, Lazare de Baïf (1485–1545 or 1547) and Christophe de Longueil (1488–1522) mounted a challenge to Budé's hitherto undisputed mastery of Greek prose composition.[29] However, the Greek letters they exchanged left Budé's linguistic primacy safe. Here Le Roy briefly interrupted the chronicle of Budé's life to insert an encomium to his late-flowering genius, and when he resumed his narrative, he had Budé once more start up from a position of weakness. In the second narrative section, Le Roy recounted how Budé's excessive devotion to philology caused him to suffer from chronic migraines.[30] Following Budé's account of his illness in his letters to various people including his physician, Le Roy described how these headaches impeded his progress in scholarship as well as prompting his father's ire: Jean Budé begged his son to abandon humanism in favour of managing his financial affairs, but Budé obstinately refused to forsake his studies.

Despite his illness and paternal opposition, he persevered with his study of Greek. After his father's death, he began to publish translations of some of Plutarch's moral essays, followed by original works, such as the legal commentary *Annotationes ... in Pandectas* (*Annotations on the Pandects*, 1508) which established his reputation in western Europe.[31] Thereafter, his flow of publications continued unchecked until a second major crisis — this time international in scale — broke out with the quarrel over the authorship of his most famous scholarly work, a treatise on ancient coinage, weights and measures entitled *De Asse* (1515; the *as* was a Roman coin). Budé emerged with reputation intact, just as he had done from the first crisis. Still, Le Roy marked the greater magnitude of this second crisis by emphasizing how its resolution depended on the intervention of several other scholars; Longueil and Baïf, by contrast, had graciously admitted defeat on their own. Le Roy devoted the following several pages to a discussion of the rumoured rivalry between the two giants of northern humanism, Budé and Erasmus. This rivalry threatened to develop into a third crisis, but instead found resolution in a declaration of their complementarity and friendship.[32]

The *Vita* culminated with a final and far more serious crisis which affected the entire community of humanists, by threatening the status of 'bonæ litteræ'. According to Le Roy, the church authorities blamed the study of Greek for the outbreak of heresy rapidly gaining momentum in the 1530s. As a result of the association between the study of ancient languages and the religious Reform movement, church and crown together undertook the persecution of humanists across France. However, because of Budé's pre-eminent stature, he alone amongst scholars escaped unscathed. Just before the end of the *Vita*, Le Roy temporarily abandoned the narrative to indulge in a final digression, an elaborate set-piece in praise of François I as patron of learning. This eulogy forms a pendant to the account of Budé's own life, setting it in its broader historical context. Le Roy followed up this pæan with a brief concluding narrative of Budé's final illness and death in the king's service.

Le Roy's compositional technique, then, shows considerable sophistication as we see from this synopsis of the *Vita*. In structural terms, its plot resembles an ever broadening spiral which tracks its hero from crisis to crisis, each one with more serious ramifications. This cyclical movement simultaneously describes an upward trajectory with Budé progressing in both scholarship and general esteem. Thus the formal structure of the *Vita* clearly foreshadows the *Vicissitude*'s philosophy of history which similarly fused cyclicality with linearity and progress.

A striking echo of this idea of progress as movement spiralling both outwards and upwards reverberates in a vivid image Le Roy used in the preface to his 1558 translation of Plato's *Symposium*, to convey his view that only by imitating the great writers of the past could contemporaries achieve excellence and fame:

> Car comme l'hierre s'entortillant à quelque fort arbre croissant, s'eleve ensemble et parcroist: ainsi ensuyvant et imitant les excellens ouvriers, lon se dresse peu à peu, et vient lon à quelque perfection et reputation.

The same preoccupation with imitation as a motor driving progress, instanced here, also furnished the *Vita* with its key unifying theme, one which circles round the story of Budé's life just as the twisting ivy imaged in the quoted text winds itself round a great tree. Each of the crises shaping its plot deals with a problem related to imitation as a spur to ever greater scholarly achievement or to envy as an obstacle choking it. Thus Le Roy's story of Budé's exemplary life reads as a moral drama which treats of the substitution of envy ('invidia') with its positive counterpart, emulation ('æmulatio'): where envy seeks to destroy, emulation drives innovation through self-discovery.

Le Roy set the stage for this drama in the biography proper with a prefatory diatribe, warning against the ravages caused by envy amongst scholars in the contemporary age.[33] At the same time, Le Roy announced his seemingly contradictory goal of presenting the life of a uniquely irreproducible personality as a model for the reader to imitate. This paradoxical quality of the exemplary figure — understood at once as a rare exception to the norm and a reproducible phenomenon — typifies the early modern rhetoric of exemplarity.[34] Motivated by a feeling of community with all men of letters, he declared his desire to create a likeness of the model humanist 'not only to gaze upon, but indeed to be imitated' ('non solum ad intuendum, verumetiam ad imitandum'). Le Roy's invocation of the need for practical application on the part of the reader is similarly in keeping with the modalities of Renaissance exemplarity.[35] But he also warned that failure could all too easily result from such temerity, so completely did Budé tower over all other scholars:

> [...] it is amazing, how greatly Budé alone should excel, whether we consider his understanding and knowledge of Greek and Latin, or of the noble arts and of abstruse matters, or whether we look at the integrity of his life, or indeed his great works of genius.[36]

Happily, Le Roy presented the reader with an internal model of an alternative, mediated form of imitation. Rather than trying to copy Budé directly, the aspiring humanist could instead learn from the experience of other characters in the biography who had themselves attempted, with varying degrees of success, to fashion themselves in Budé's image or who had unwisely challenged his pre-eminence by claiming his original achievements for themselves.

Biographers from Plutarch onwards had asserted that the value of their works lay in their presentation of models of virtue to imitate or of vices to avoid. As Plutarch declared in the preface to his *Life of Pericles*:

> Moral good, in a word, has a power to attract towards itself. It is no sooner seen than it rouses the spectator to action, and yet it does not form his character by mere imitation, but by promoting the understanding of virtuous deeds it provides him with a dominating purpose.[37]

Le Roy likewise specified that he had undertaken the biography of Budé with the same ethical goals in mind as those of his ancient precursors.[38] In the preface to the *Vita*, Le Roy, like most humanistic biographers, gestured at behavioural rather than literary imitation ('imitatio'), or imitation as a pedagogic method.[39] Thus he invoked Budé's character ('mores') rather than his literary technique or intellectual formation:

> In addition, when they consider his way of life, nature, character, severity, steadfastness, excellence, and prudence, they will also understand what I consider to be especially beneficial and profitable in these times, that without doubt integrity of character rather than display of knowledge should be sought from the cultivation of letters.[40]

As I have observed, Le Roy structured the entire biography around the dynamic interplay of 'æmulatio' and 'invidia', making it a key text for the representation of exemplarity in the period. Although Budé himself remained immune to the latter passion, others did repeatedly impute him with experiencing it. And he continuously attracted the envy of his fellow humanists with ever more serious consequences. Both 'invidia' and 'æmulatio' first appear in the *Vita* when the young Christophe de Longueil attempted to persuade Budé to take him on as a beginning pupil in Greek. On being refused, Longueil accused Budé of being jealous of his own reputation and not wishing anyone else to have the chance to rival it.[41] According to Le Roy's account, Longueil speculated that Budé had rejected him as a student because he did not wish to train a future rival who might eventually share in his glory.[42] Longueil thus ascribed to Budé a defensive kind of envy which attached itself to the mere possibility of another scholar's achievement, since he had not even learned Greek when he first approached the elder humanist.

However, Longueil only mistakenly suspected that Budé might envy his potential accomplishments in Greek. In reality, Le Roy emphasized that Budé at no point fell under envy's sway. As it transpired, the encounter between Longueil and Budé did not ultimately generate envy but instead its positive counterpart: 'æmulatio'.[43] While Longueil never did manage to surpass his model, he nonetheless had a modicum of success as a Hellenist, sending Budé a Greek letter which the elder scholar praised for its charm.[44] Budé too benefited, as his fame increased when he replied to this missive with an even more elegantly composed letter. Still, Longueil failed to advance scholarship when he attempted to make himself into another Budé as he could never duplicate his singular excellence in Greek prose composition. For the reader of the *Vita*, then, the real lesson of Longueil's experience must lie elsewhere.

This episode teaches us that imitation, in the sense of transforming oneself into an exact copy of one's model, represents a scholarly dead end. Instead, it substitutes for such a mechanical notion of 'imitatio' another, more productive way of relating to the exemplar. Just what this way might be emerges from careful evaluation of the nature of Longueil's request and of Budé's response to it. Longueil asked Budé to instruct him in Greek, and specified his preferred teaching method: daily sessions during which his teacher would read aloud from Greek texts — precisely the kind of instruction which had initially proved disastrous for Budé.[45] Budé's first teacher of Greek, George Hermonymus of Sparta, read aloud to him from Homer, assiduously (though for a fee), every day for a number of years without any demonstrable benefit to his pupil.[46] So Budé's refusal to oblige Longueil — on the ostensible grounds that family and other business had a prior claim on his time — seems charitable when we take into account this earlier experience. However, Budé did also make a very reasonable counter-proposal to Longueil. Specifically, he suggested that Longueil should rely primarily on his own resources, just as the autodidact Budé himself had done, and gave permission to consult him from a distance if he ran into difficulties — again, as Budé had profitably done with his second teacher, Jean Lascaris (1454–1535).[47] Thus, Budé effectively counselled Longueil to adopt his pedagogic model of independent self-reliance as a means to develop his own excellence.

Unfortunately, Budé's offer of a correspondence course in Greek did not satisfy Longueil. Instead, he conspired with his friend Lazare de Baïf to go to Italy where he hoped to acquire an even better Greek than Budé's because of the presence of superior teachers and richer libraries.[48] In announcing Longueil's project of studying in Italy, Le Roy set up a strong antithesis which emphasized the contrast between Budé and the hapless young upstart:

> that man [Budé], taught entirely by himself, had made great progress in Greek, and in all the branches of the liberal arts; as for himself, he [Longueil] would find everything far better equipped for learning in terms of opportunity and teachers.[49]

Le Roy thereby intimated that Longueil failed in his mimetic rivalry precisely because he failed to take Budé's advice and rely on his own resources. By deviating from the guidance Budé offered, Longueil wound up falling hopelessly short of the mark in his quest to imitate the great scholar.

But Longueil's journey to Italy did ultimately yield a positive outcome, despite initial indications to the contrary. When he finally had to acknowledge his failure to surpass Budé as a Hellenist, he renounced Greek studies altogether.[50] His story points out a potential risk of 'æmulatio' as a motor of scholarly progress: the failure of imitation to yield the desired results may lead to a realization of the impossibility of surpassing one's model and to the abandonment of a project. In which case, the imitation of the exemplary personality might just as easily be said to threaten as inspire the spread of excellence. Biographies of men such as Budé would only exacerbate this problem by luring would-be imitators. However, Le Roy's account of Longueil's experience does in fact validate the exemplary figure as a means of fostering excellence in others: Budé's abilities remained singular (imitative rivalry only increased his quota of praise within the scholarly community) but through 'æmulatio' Longueil found another area in which he could personally excel, emerging from his confrontation with Budé with a claim to first place as a Latinist.[51] Were it not for Longueil's untimely death, he might have been, in his own way, another Budé. Although his bid to copy Budé did not yield the initially desired results, Longueil's discovery of his own true excellence came via the more flexible notion of 'æmulatio'. Only through creative 'imitatio', through fashioning oneself against a model, can one discover one's individuality.

Indeed, both this model of 'imitatio' and Longueil's genius find further recognition within the *Vita* itself, as Le Roy went on to quote at some length the famous Latin letter in which that scholar compared the unique styles of Budé and Erasmus.[52] This letter, Le Roy noted, should teach apprentice orators what to admire and imitate in both men, following the eclectic school of imitation advocated most notably first by Angelo Poliziano (1454–94) and later by Pico della Mirandola (1470–1533).[53] Earlier in this section of the *Vita*, moreover, Le Roy had argued for an idea of style as an expression of personal temperament, such as that advocated by the sensible Bulephorus in Erasmus's 1528 *Ciceronianus* — a frontal attack on the Ciceronians, exclusive imitators of Cicero's Latin, with none other than Longueil as its putative object of caricature.[54] Longueil's fervent and well-known commitment to Ciceronianism makes his role in the *Vita* as the spokesperson for a very different brand of 'imitatio' highly ironic.[55] Longueil's Ciceronianism had contributed to the estrangement between Budé and Erasmus, which Le Roy also neglected to discuss. He nowhere mentioned Budé's apparent coldness regarding Longueil, as evidenced by his less than grief-stricken reaction to that scholar's death.[56] This had misled Erasmus into believing that Budé might be his ally against the Ciceronians.[57] After the publication of Erasmus's *Ciceronianus*, however, Budé disappointed this expectation.[58]

When in 1514 Budé published what would become his most famous work of original scholarship, the numismatic treatise *De asse*, a second, more serious outbreak of 'invidia' erupted. Le Roy stressed both the excellence of this work and its vulnerability to the envy of other scholars:

> But such an elegant, finished, painstakingly crafted work could not have escaped envy and disparagement. A fair number of people emerged who rather than delighting in its excellence, took offence at its brilliance. Such persons preferred to undermine with their envy a work which they ought to have approved with their praise [...] [59]

With this episode, Le Roy demonstrated how envy, when not converted into productive emulation, could threaten scholarly progress.[60] He urged humanists to work together to safeguard their community from the ravages of 'invidia'. Recalling his discussion in the preface, Le Roy suggested that the envy to which Budé's *De asse* fell prey derived from the insidious overall moral character of the times.[61] But Le Roy needed a villain to enhance the dramatic value of this conflict and he found one in the person of the little known Italian lawyer–scholar Leonardo Porzio (or Portius, 1460–1545). Porzio did not publish his very similar work, the *De sestertio*, until 1524, nearly a decade after the first edition of the *De asse*, but it had circulated in Rome in a manuscript version some years previously.[62] Just as Longueil had done, Porzio levelled against the great Budé the accusation of not wishing to share his glory. Indeed, Porzio made so bold as to ascribe to himself an equal share in Budé's glory as co-author of the *De asse*. Whereas the young Longueil had earlier charged Budé with refusing a potential future partner in glory, this time, however, the fully-fledged rival humanist Porzio presented himself as Budé's equal. As we soon discover, this dispute proved even more dangerous to Budé's status than the previous one. Only speciously, even, did Porzio propose that the two scholars share in their glory. In reality, he sought to appropriate for himself all the glory of the *De asse* and its key discovery which helped to unlock the ancient system of weights and measures: namely that ancient writers regularly omitted the multiplier 'centena millia' from figures such as 'decies centena millia sestertium'.[63] Having published essentially the same book as his rival, Porzio could legitimately claim an intellectual stature more closely equal to Budé's than could Longueil, as the latter knew but a negligible amount of Greek when he approached the senior scholar. Because of Budé's and Porzio's comparable status, envy presented an altogether more intractable problem.

Their dispute, however, cast into doubt not only Budé's claim to the sole authorship of the *De asse* and thus his scholarly reputation (his 'gloria'), but more crucially, his moral integrity. Budé responded to Porzio's threat with anger, whereas previously with Longueil he had merely shown first obduracy, in refusing to teach him (although this may have been out of benevolence), and later politeness, in his epistolary response to Longueil's Greek letters. The resolution of this impasse between rival Hellenists depended on the mediation of several fellow scholars (namely the Greek scholar and Budé's fellow royal librarian Jean Lascaris, 1445–1535, the prominent Venetian humanist Baptista Egnazio, *c.*1473–1553, and the German scholar and scientist Georg Agricola, 1494–1555). Only when Lascaris compelled Budé to retract a vicious digression criticizing Porzio from the 1527 edition of the *De asse*,[64] did the crisis abate. Egnazio also defused the tension by praising both men equally in a preface to his edition of Suetonius.

In the *Vita*, Le Roy gave an accurate enough, if simplified version of this disagreement. In actual fact, in addition to the three scholars Le Roy mentioned, the protracted, convoluted quarrel involved Longueil and the Italian jurist Andrea Alciati (1492–1550) as well, both of whom intervened to reconcile the disputants. Effectively an intensification of the clash with Longueil, the conflict over the authorship of the *De asse* pitted Budé against a single challenger in a scholarly duel of forces. International in scale, this dispute set Budé and the exponents of northern humanism against the Italians. Le Roy, in keeping with his general practice in the *Vita*, glossed over Budé's chauvinistic anti-Italianism. He also compressed the sixteen-year timescale of the affair, so as to make the exemplary Budé's recognition of his moral weakness in succumbing to the passion of anger, and his subsequent self-correction, seem more rapid. Le Roy allowed that Budé did initially get angry with Porzio, but he concluded his account by stating the French humanist's stoic resolution never to become embroiled in a scholarly spat again. And Le Roy made abundantly clear that Budé and his allies had vanquished Porzio, as his French hero thoroughly eclipsed his Italian rival's scholarly reputation: envy always destroyed the invidious. For his part, after this episode, Budé withdrew entirely from the battlefield, never again to be touched by envy.[65]

And so, when a third and yet graver crisis cast its shadow over Greek studies — involving not the malice of envious individuals but the group persecution of humanists by church and crown — Budé alone remained unaffected by it, such was his undisputed pre-eminence.[66] In the aftermath of this final episode, Le Roy described how admiring scholars began to come from far and wide to seek Budé's approbation for their works. By this point in the *Vita*, we have come full circle from Longueil and Baïf's envy-propelled flight into Italy. Budé's stature was now such that he attracted the emulation of a distinguished community of scholars without the threat of envy. Thus Le Roy's *Vita* dramatized how, despite the external difficulties of persecution by the royal and ecclesiastical authorities, Budé's triumph over invidiousness and personal enmity had created a milieu in which general scholarly endeavour could flourish, at least in the safe haven of his immediate circle.

Le Roy published his *Vita* as a young courtier in search of a patron. He succeeded in attracting the attention of its dedicatee, the then powerful chancellor, Poyet. As Budé's own patron and friend, Poyet would no doubt have been touched by Le Roy's pious admiration for a great scholar who had held considerable influence over François I's cultural policy. But Le Roy's biography did not merely seal Budé's reputation as France's greatest humanist, whose qualities rivalled those of the redoubtable Erasmus. Rather, it announced Le Roy's own ambitions as a budding scholar, by introducing certain key ideas about cultural history which would find their full flowering in his mature masterwork, *De la vicissitude*. In addition to narrating Budé's life, Le Roy used the *Vita* as a pretext for discussions of the contemporary cultural scene, placed in the preface and in a lengthy digression near the end of the text. In these passages, he articulated a view of human civilization as subject to alternating periods of growth and decline. His optimistic modernism also shone through as he heaped praise on the achievements of his own day as surpassing those of the ancients. Envious rivalry between contemporary scholars represented the only cloud in the sky. Budé himself would most likely have endorsed Le Roy's observations as the two men shared much the same view of civilization.[67] Le Roy's philosophy of cultural history, though, permeated his narration of Budé's life as well. As presented by Le Roy, Budé's career oscillated between periods of expansion and contraction, following an overall upward vector. Such a pattern also injected a welcome element of drama into the biography.

Still, Le Roy did not develop his position as a cultural historian to the full until some thirty years later, once he had secured a post as Royal Professor of Greek. This position afforded him the stability to produce his encyclopaedic history of human civilization, the *Vicissitude*, a work whose digressive style relates it to Budé's own expression of humanism. This text, and a shorter preparatory sketch for it, the *Consideration sur l'histoire françoise et universelle de ce temps* (1567), take up once again the thread of Le Roy's historical thought first announced in the *Vita*.[68] The intervening years he spent as a wandering courtier, a scholar in want of a reliable Maecenas, serving a long apprenticeship as French translator, most notably of Plato. Le Roy's translations earned him the acclaim of his contemporaries. But the problem of how to convert oneself from translator and journeyman humanist, one who imitated the works of his predecessors as a means of training his own pen ('afin de dresser par imitation le style et jugement sur eux'), into master scholar constantly preoccupied Le Roy, as several of the prefaces to his versions attest.

The *Vita* dramatized this concern too by portraying Budé as an exemplary figure who might serve as a model for conduct and a guide to action. Le Roy's account offered its readers a model for how beginning humanists might make progress and measure themselves against so great a scholar as Budé. The community of men of letters should avoid envy at all costs. Rather, as the *Vita* suggests, a particular form of the pedagogic method of 'imitatio' represented the best way for the next generation of humanists to find their own excellence through creative emulation. Le Roy's own career, which echoed that of Budé in an admittedly minor key, exemplifies this. Behind Le Roy's interest in a hybrid form of literary and behavioural imitation though — the latter a commonplace of biographical rhetoric from antiquity onwards — we can detect his preoccupation with how to use his association with Budé to establish himself as an intellectual in his own right. The *Vita* formed a crucial element in Le Roy's bid to convert his status as an apprentice humanist and translator into that of an original scholar, capable of producing philosophical works which could stand alongside those of the ancients he admired. In order to make his biography of Budé serve this purpose, Le Roy used this text to adumbrate his philosophy of history and prepare the ground for his masterpiece, the *Vicissitude*.

But Le Roy's transformation of himself into a worthy successor to Budé did not follow automatically from the publication of the *Vita*. During the twenty years following the publication of the *Vita*, Le Roy would continue to operate as a courtier and confine himself almost exclusively to translations rather than produce original works. So Le Roy's defence of literary imitation in the preface to his 1559 translation of Plato's *Symposium* entailed an apologia for his own prodigious activities as a translator during the 1550s. He made translations from the Greek to refine his style and judgement 'selon le temps ou nous vivons, *et ma portée*' [emphasis mine]'. Le Roy thus differentiated his brand of imitation from the slavish form so reviled by theorists of 'imitatio'; for him, translation represented a vital intermediary step on the way to producing original works.[69] By 1560, however, Le Roy had established his reputation as a humanist amongst fellow scholars on the strength of his translations from Greek into the vernacular.[70] Nonetheless, as he made clear in the same preface to the *Sympose*, Le Roy had far greater ambitions for himself as a scholar. However beneficial translation from Greek might be for the sixteenth-century French reading public, Le Roy conceded that such activity ultimately had less intellectual value than the production of new works:

> Vray est que le traduire de soy et transcrire simplement d'un livre en l'autre, n'est tant louable qu'il est penible, et vauldroit trop mieux mettre en avant ses propres inventions, qui a moyen de le faire.[71]

As a 'courtisan vagabond' turned royal professor, Le Roy's professional tenacity finally secured him the means to produce original works near the end of his life. The *Vita* served him as a launch pad for a type of career which Budé's own sustained promotion of humanism at the court of François I made possible for a young man like Le Roy to pursue.[72]

Notes to Chapter 1

1. Louis Le Roy, *Gulielmi Budæi Vita per Ludovicum Regium, ad Gulielmum Poietum magnum Franciæ cancellarium* (= *GBV*) (Paris: Jean Roigny 1540, re-edition 1542). The *GBV* also appears in Budé, *Opera omnia*, ed. by Celio Secondo Curione (Basel: N. Episcopius, 1557) (= *OO*). In what follows, unless otherwise specified, I refer to the *GBV* and to Budé's works in the 1966 reprint of the *OO* (Farnborough, Hants: Gregg Press). *GBV*, fol. FF 4v°.
2. Budé's 1535 *De transitu Hellenismi ad Christianisimum* (*Passage from Hellenism to Christianity*) best illustrates his thought on this question. See Marie-Madeleine de La Garanderie, 'Guillaume Budé, a Philosopher of Culture', *The Sixteenth Century Journal*, 19 (1988), 379–87 (pp. 380–82).
3. Budé wrote frequently about the tension between his civic role and his studies, generally to stress his disinterest in material wealth and courtly life. See Budé, *De Philologia* (*On Philology*, 1532), *OO*, fol. 91; *De studio literarum recte et commode instituendo* (*The Ways of Right Learning*, 1532), *OO*, fols. 8–9; Erasmus, *Opus epistolarum Des. Erasmi Roterdami*, ed. by Percy S. Allen, 12 vols (Oxford : Clarendon Press, 1906–58), II, 522 lns 58–60; Gadoffre, *La Révolution culturelle*, pp. 69–72; David O. McNeil, *Guillaume Budé and Humanism in the Reign of Francis I* (Geneva: Droz, 1975), pp. 47–60 and pp. 96–97. Still, McNeil rightly emphasizes that, despite his internal conflict, Budé took an active role in royal politics and that, as the owner of two country properties, at Saint-Maur and Marly, he left his family far from impoverished. In a Greek letter of 19 January 1517 to his brother Louis, Budé's proclaims his scorn for excessive wealth. The same letter however also contains Budé's offer to help his sibling perfect his mastery of Greek in exchange for lessons in estate management to ensure a decent standard of living for his growing family (*OO*, fols. 402–05). Cited in McNeil, *Budé*, p. 85. Translation in Budé, *Correspondance. Tome 1. Les Lettres grecques*, ed. by Guy Lavoie (Sherbrooke, Quebec: Centre d'Etudes de la Renaissance, 1977), pp. 87–97.
4. Born into a wealthy landowning family whose nobility dated to the early fourteenth century, Budé belonged to a line of magistrates who occupied high positions in the royal bureaucracy. Gerald Sandy, 'Guillaume Budé: Philologist and Polymath: A Preliminary Study', in *The Classical Heritage in France* (Leiden: Brill, 2002), pp. 79–108 (p. 81).
5. On Poyet, see Charles Porée, *Un parlementaire sous François Ier: Guillaume Poyet (1473–1548)* (Angers: Germain et G. Grassin, 1898). On Poyet and Budé's sons, see ibid., p. 98. Budé's letter of 8 May 1519 to Dreux expresses paternal concern for the family's future standing, albeit primarily conceived of in terms of reputation for intellectual achievement. Nonetheless Budé concludes the missive by exhorting Dreux to acquire the social graces that will allow him to mix in worldly circles (*OO*, fols. 285–87). Gadoffre, *Révolution*, p. 84.
6. *GBV*, fol. EE2r°.
7. On Toussain, appointed Lecteur royal of Greek in 1529, see McNeil, *Budé*, p. 86.
8. Montaigne accused him of being unable to compose a decent Latin harangue. Michel de Montaigne, *Les Essais*, ed. by Pierre Villey, 3rd corrected edn, 3 vols (Paris: Presses universitaires françaises, 1999), I, 10, p. 39. Cited by Jean Dupèbe, 'Un chancelier humaniste sous François

Ier: François Olivier (1497–1560)', in *Humanism and Letters in the Age of François Ier*, ed. by Philip Ford and Gillian Jondorf (Cambridge: Cambridge French Colloquia, 1996), pp. 87–114 (p. 88). On his contemporaries' vitriolic attacks against Poyet, see ibid., p. 88, n. 5.

9. McNeil, *Budé*, p. 108; Porée, *Un parlementaire*, p. 97.
10. A. Henri Becker, *Un Humaniste au XVIe siècle: Loys Le Roy de Coutances* (Paris: Oudin, 1896), p. 8.
11. On Le Roy's ineptitude as a courtier, see Becker, *Un humaniste au XVIe siècle*, pp. 8–18. Le Roy succinctly outlined his career in the preface to the reader of his translation of Plato's *Symposium* (Paris: Vincent Sertenas, 1559). See also Philippe Desan, *Penser l'histoire à la renaissance* (Caen: Paradigme, 1993), pp. 171–74; Werner L. Gundersheimer, *The Life and Works of Louis Le Roy* (Geneva: Droz, 1966), pp. 10–29.
12. Le Roy also notably translated the digression on hunting in Budé's *De Philologia* (fols. 43v°–59v°). Prepared for Charles IX in 1572, Le Roy's *Traité de la venerie* circulated only in manuscript until the nineteenth century, however.
13. Sandy, 'Philologist and Polymath', p. 88. Budé also translated the same author's *De tranquilitate animi* (*On tranquillity of mind*, 1501) and dedicated it to Pope Julius I. The significance of these versions of Plutarch's essays notwithstanding, translation formed a far less important part of Budé's scholarly output than it did of Le Roy's.
14. See, for example, *De l'excellence du gouvernement royal* (1575). McNeil, *Budé*, pp. 37–48; Gundersheimer, *Le Roy*, pp. 67–79.
15. Donald Kelley, *Foundations of Modern Historical Scholarship: Language, Law and History in the French Renaissance* (New York: Columbia University Press, 1970), p. 81.
16. Although royal secretary since the 1490s thanks to his father's intervention, Budé did not exercise this function until decades later. The office of 'maître des requêtes' he earned through his own years of service to François I. McNeil, *Budé*, pp. 93–94.
17. Kelley, *Foundations*, p. 58.
18. Gundersheimer, *Le Roy*, p. 60 and p. 106.
19. Desan, *Penser l'histoire*, p. 175; Jacques Chomarat, *Prosateurs latins en France au XVIe siècle* (Paris: Presses de la Sorbonne, 1987), p. 477.
20. Kelley, *Foundations*, p. 81. On Budé and Le Roy's shared penchant for close observation of cultural, historical and linguistic details, see Sandy, 'Philologist and Polymath', p. 85. In books 1 and 4 of *De asse* (1515), Budé also argued that all nations could potentially attain a high degree of culture and civilization. La Garanderie, *Christianisme & lettres profanes. Essai sur l'Humanisme français (1515–1535) et sur la pensée de Guillaume Budé* (Paris: H. Champion, 1995), p. 220. Le Roy advanced a parallel argument in *Vicissitude*, fol. 29v°.
21. Desan, *Penser l'histoire*, p. 175.
22. Erasmus critically likened Budé to a 'wealthy householder who wants to put all his possessions on display'. Allen, II, 480, lns 214–42. Cited in Sandy, 'Philologist and polymath', p. 93. On Budé's digressions, see also ibid., pp. 102–05.
23. Allen, II, 583. *De Philologia*, *OO*, fols. 34–38. See Michel Magnien, 'Portrait de Budé en "intellectuel": la *G. Budæi viri clarissimi vita* de Loys Le Roy (1540)', *Renaissance and Reformation* 24.4 (2000), 29–48 (p. 31 and p. 41, n.18).
24. See Paul Barolsky, *Michelangelo's Nose: A Myth and its Maker* (University Park: Pennsylvania State University Press, 1990) on the similar function of the Condivi and Vasari *Lives* of Michelangelo.
25. Kelley, *Foundations*, p. 83.
26. Gundersheimer, *Le Roy*, p. 107.
27. Allen, II, 583, lns. 380–84.
28. Magnien draws attention to the resemblance between the *Vita* and the conversion narratives which feature in many saints' lives ('Portrait', p. 31).
29. On Baïf, see Lucien Pinvert, *Lazare de Baïf (1496?–1547)* (Paris: A. Fontemoing, 1900); on Longueil, Théophile Simar, *Christophe de Longueil, Humaniste* (Louvain: Bureaux du Recueil, 1911).
30. Guy Lavoie, 'G. Budé à son médecin. Un inédit sur sa maladie', *Renaissance and Reformation/ Renaissance et Réforme*, n.s. 15.1 (1991), 37–56 cites all the relevant letters. Magnien, 'Portrait', p. 33.

31. Sandy, 'Philologist and Polymath', p. 83.
32. On the vicissitudes in the relations between Budé and Erasmus, see McNeil, *Budé*, pp. 61–76.
33. *GBV*, fol. EE 2.
34. Lyons, *Exemplum*, p. 11 and pp. 32–33.
35. Hampton, *Writing from History*, p. 10.
36. '[...] admirabile est, quantum Budæus unus excellat, sive utriusque linguæ cognitionem, sive magnarum artium, et reconditarum rerum scientiam, sive vitæ integritatem, sive præclara ingenii monumenta, spectemus'. *GBV*, fol. EE 2 r°.
37. Plutarch, 'Pericles', in *The Rise and Fall of Athens*, p. 166.
38. *GBV*, EE2r°.
39. Hampton (*Writing from History*, pp. 4–5) and Lyons (*Exemplum*, p. 12) discuss the nexus of these two concepts of imitation. On the range of Renaissance conceptions of imitation see for example Ann Moss, 'Literary imitation in the sixteenth century: writers and readers, Latin and French', in *The Cambridge History of Literary Criticism. Volume III. The Renaissance*, ed. by G. P. Norton (Cambridge: Cambridge University Press, 1999), pp. 107–18; Martin L. McLaughlin, *Literary Imitation in the Renaissance: The Theory and Practice of Literary Imitation in Italy from Dante to Bembo* (Oxford: Clarendon Press, 1995); and Thomas M. Greene, *The Light in Troy: Imitation and Discovery in Renaissance Poetry* (New Haven, CT: Yale University Press, 1982).
40. 'Ad hæc cum genus vitæ, naturam, mores, gravitatem, constantiam, præstantiam, atque prudentiam intuebuntur, id quoque intelligent quod præcipue his temporibus salubre et frugiferum existimo, nempe ex literis non ostentationem scientiæ, sed integritatem morum multo magis esse quærendam'. *GBV*, fol. EE2v°.
41. *GBV*, fol. EE 3 v°.
42. *GBV*, fol. EE 3 v°.
43. This contradicts the desperate situation Le Roy described in the preface where he declared that envy irredeemably marred the contemporary age. (*GBV*, fol. EE 2r°).
44. Their Greek correspondence features together with Budé's other Greek letters in: *Epistolæ Gulielmi Budæi, Secretarii Regii.* (Paris: J. Bade, 1520); *Epistolæ Gulielmi Budæi, Secretarii Regii. Posteriores.* (Paris: J. Bade, 1522); *G. Budæi...epistolarum latinarum lib. V. Annotationibusque adjectis in singulas fere epistolas. Græcarum item lib. I.* (Paris: J. Bade, 1531).
45. *GBV*, fol. EE 3v°.
46. *GBV*, fol. EE 3r°. On Hermonymus, see McNeil, *Budé*, pp. 10–12 and Henri Omont, *George Hermonyme de Sparte, maître de grec à Paris* (Paris: Nogent-le-Rotrou, 1885), pp. 5–11. Budé complained specifically in the 1517 letter to Cuthbert Tunstall of Hermonymus's oral rather than text-based method of instruction. Allen, II, 583, lns 395–420.
47. Lascaris's diplomatic activities meant that he was frequently away from Paris, but he agreed to give Budé what assistance he could (*GBV*, fol. EE 3r°). See Börje Knös, *Un ambassadeur de l'hellénisme, Janus Lascaris et la tradition gréco-byzantine dans l'humanisme français* (Uppsala and Stockholm: Almqvist & Wiksells, 1945), pp. 84–93.
48. On Baïf and this journey to Italy, see Pinvert, *Baïf*, pp. 6–11.
49. 'illum a seipso edoctum tantum processisse in literis Græcis, et omni arte ingenua et liberalique doctrina: sibi facultatem, sibi magistros, sibi denique paratiora omnia ad discendum fore'. *GBV*, fol. EE 3v°.
50. *GBV*, fol. EE 3v°.
51. *GBV*, fol. EE 3v°.
52. See the detailed analysis of this section of the *GBV* in Marc Fumaroli, *L'Age de l'éloquence. Rhétorique et «res literaria» au seuil de l'époque classique* (Geneva: Droz, 1980), pp. 446–50.
53. McLaughlin, *Literary Imitation*, pp. 249–74.
54. *GBV*, fol. EE 6r°. Greene, *Light*, p. 182.
55. On Le Roy's own Ciceronianism, see Becker, *Un Humaniste au XVIe siècle*, p. 42; and Gundersheimer, *Le Roy*, p. 59.
56. 'Longolium olim nostrum luctuosius desiderassem, nisi ipse noster esse, id est Francus, animi destinatione desiisset'. Allen, VII, 1812, lns 136–37.
57. See Allen, VII, 1840, esp. lns 84–87.
58. For a complete account of events surrounding the publication of the *Ciceronianus*, and the breakdown in relations between Budé and Erasmus, see McNeil, *Budé*, pp. 69–75.

59. 'Sed opus tam elegans, tam perfectum, tam elaboratum effugere non potuit invidiam et obtrectationem. Inventique sunt nonnulli, quos non tam præstantia eius delectaret, quam splendor offenderet. qui quod laudando debuerant comprobare, invidendo infringere maluerunt [...]'. *GBV*, fol. EE 5 v°.
60. *GBV*, fol. EE 5v°.
61. *GBV*, fol. EE 5v°.
62. La Garanderie, *Christianisme*, p. 78; McNeil, *Budé*, p. 29.
63. McNeil, *Budé*, p. 29.
64. Paris, 1527. See Katharine Davies, 'Leonardo Porzio in the 1527 *De asse*', in *Acta Conventus neo-latini Bononiensis*, ed. Richard J. Schoeck (Binghampton, NY: Centre for Medieval and Renaissance Studies, State University of New York, 1985), pp. 430–36.
65. For statements of Budé's subsequent docility, see *GBV*, fol. EE 5v°; *GBV*, fol. FF 1v°.
66. *GBV*, fol. FF 2v°.
67. Kelley, *Foundations*, pp. 80–82.
68. See Bodo L. O. Richter, 'The Thought of Louis Le Roy according to his Early Pamphlets', *Studies in the Renaissance*, 8 (1961), 173–96.
69. Du Bellay, *Deffense et illustration de la langue françoyse*, in *Œuvres complètes*, ed. by Francis Goyet and Olivier Millet, 2 vols (Paris: H. Champion, 2003–), I, 26–29; Greene, *Light in Troy*, pp. 51–53.
70. Desan, *Penser l'histoire*, p. 172.
71. Greene provides a survey of contemporary critiques of imitation, from Montaigne ('Qui suit un autre, il ne suit rien, il ne trouve rien, voire il ne cherche rien') to Johnson (*Light in Troy*, p. 44).
72. On Budé as an advocate of humanism and philology, see Sandy, 'Philologist and Polymath', pp. 106–08 and McNeil, *Budé*, p. 130.

Figure 2. Portrait of Pibrac from Charles Paschal, *La Vie et mœurs de messire Guy du Faur, seigneur de Pybrac*, tr. by Guy du Faur, seigneur d'Hermay (Paris: Thibault du Val, 1617), p. 2. © The British Library Board. All Rights Reserved. 609.a.11.(2.)

CHAPTER 2

❖

Diplomacy and Biography in the Wars of Religion: Charles Paschal's Life of Guy du Faur de Pibrac (1584)

Like Le Roy's *Vita Budæi*, Charles Paschal's (Carlo Pasquale, or Carolus Paschalius, 1547–1625) biography of his first patron, the magistrate, diplomat and poet, Guy du Faur de Pibrac (1529–84), appeared in the year of its subject's death.[1] As with the former text, its composition in Latin enabled it to reach a European readership. Such an international audience was certainly appropriate for the life of Pibrac, a career diplomat whose missions had taken him to Germany, Italy and Poland. Its author too, had an equally cosmopolitan profile: Paschal, Piedmontese by birth, owed his introduction to the French court to Pibrac, whose support subsequently also earned him a number of important royal commissions both in France and elsewhere in Europe.

Paschal's biography gives an unequivocally laudatory account of Pibrac as a moderate Catholic and a conservative royalist who successfully pursued a career in three royal administrations over more than two decades of brutal religious wars. Alongside the generic rhetoric of praise for an exceptional statesman, Paschal also contrived to establish the specificities of Pibrac's character, qualifications and abilities as being those of a model ambassador. Paschal did this by endowing his portrait of Pibrac with a close family resemblance to depictions of the ideal ambassador found in numerous treatises by sixteenth-century theoreticians of diplomacy, for example those by Ottaviano Maggi, *De legato libri duo* (Venice, 1566, republished 1596), and Alberico Gentili, *De legationibus, libri tres* (London, 1585). Paschal himself would eventually pen two important works on diplomats and their missions: one, a practical handbook for envoys, the *Legatus* (Rouen, 1598) and the other a chronicle of his own ten-year experience as ambassador to the Swiss canton of Grisons, the *Legatio Rhetica* (Paris, 1620). His biography of Pibrac may well have nourished his scholarly reflections on this topic. But Paschal did not portray Pibrac as a model ambassador purely out of intellectual fascination with the art of diplomacy. In this chapter I shall contend that Paschal employed this representational strategy to accomplish a pragmatic aim: the cultivation of his own ambassadorial career.

Pibrac himself had nurtured this career in its earliest stages. Indeed, it was he who introduced Paschal to the Valois court when he arrived in Paris from his native Cuneo, in Piedmont, probably some time in the late 1560s or early 1570s. Of noble extraction, Paschal had come to Paris as an adolescent in order to pursue his studies, and having chosen to make his career in the French royal government he eventually became a naturalized Frenchman. In 1574–75, Pibrac may well have been instrumental in securing Paschal's first royal appointment as extraordinary ambassador to Poland. As Paschal relates in the *Pibrachii Vita*, Pibrac himself had served Henri d'Anjou faithfully when he was elected king of Poland in May 1573. On the journey eastwards, Pibrac had ridden in the royal carriage, distracting d'Anjou from his displeasure at leaving behind the charms of Paris (and more particularly those of his current mistress, the Princesse de Condé) by reading to him from Aristotle's *Politics*. More crucially, Pibrac had helped to extricate d'Anjou from Poland scarcely one year later, when news came of the death of his brother, Charles IX (1560–74), and his accession to the French throne as Henri III. Pibrac's experience would undoubtedly have counted for a great deal when it came to recommending a candidate for a subsequent Polish mission. The need for such a mission was not long in arising, for, on Henri III's precipitate return to France, the cash-strapped king had left behind certain items of valuable furniture. Their retrieval constituted Paschal's first diplomatic mission, and his success put him on the first rung of the civil servant's career. In recognition of his accomplishment, Paschal obtained the title of 'chevalier' and could add a 'fleur de lis' to his coat of arms.

On Pibrac's death, then, Paschal needed to act quickly to secure an alternative source of support. Prudence in choosing a new patron would assure the progression of his fledgling career as professional diplomat and administrator. Paschal announced his selection by dedicating the *Vita* to one of Pibrac's intimate friends, Pierre Forget, seigneur de Fresnes (1542–1610). Forget belonged to a Touraine family of which several members had served in François I's administration.[2] Considerably younger than Pibrac, Forget was much closer in age to Paschal. By the late 1570s, however, Forget already wielded considerable influence at the court of Henri III, where he had occupied a number of key offices, such as 'trésorier des parties casuelles' (royal treasurer responsible for receiving payment for venal offices) and then secretary of finance. Further prestigious offices soon followed, with Forget's appointment as royal secretary and finally 'grand audiencier de France' (first officer of the chancellery). A moderate Catholic like Pibrac, Forget nonetheless also had close ties with the Protestant Henri de Navarre, the heir presumptive to the French throne. Indeed, he had begun his career as Navarre's secretary, and had continued to act as his secret agent when he moved to the Valois court. In the tumultuous political climate of the 1580s, Forget had wisely hedged his bets and his political future looked secure in the face of any contingency. He was thus an ideal choice of patron for Paschal. Moreover, Forget had a reputation as a zealous protector of men of letters, and as a patron of arts and learning.

Paschal had only to convince Forget of his suitability as a client. To do so, he made cunning use of the dedication of his biography of Pibrac. Here, Paschal discusses the question of exemplarity in a way which provides support for Hampton's thesis of a crisis in its representation in the late sixteenth century.[3] In Hampton's assessment, this crisis saw the undermining of the authority of ancient exemplars as models of action. In similar vein, Paschal scorned examples from antiquity as having little power to move the modern reader. A contemporary author would do best to leave such superannuated *exempla* shrouded in oblivion. Examples taken from the present, on the other hand, Paschal applauded as having a tremendous potency over readers. This attitude echoes Paschal's authorial stance in his edition with commentary of the first four books of Tacitus's *Annals*. Published just three years before the *Vita*, Paschal's commentary had inaugurated the study of Tacitus as a political thinker, whose observations were especially valuable for anyone seeking to understand the behaviour of modern rulers, instead of as a historian, whose writings opened a window on to the ancient world.[4] But Paschal did not desire to champion the moderns over the ancients as a disinterested political theorist. Nor should we view this polemic in favour of the moderns as a rhetorical device to glorify Pibrac. Rather, Paschal sought to situate his biography in the present moment as an implicit means of requesting that Forget concentrate his attention on the biographer's own current predicament.

Paschal then went on to explain his motivation for writing the life narrative of Pibrac by adducing the conventional *raison d'être* for biography in this period: the provision of exemplars of virtue for imitation by the reader. As we saw in Chapter 1, biographers typically found support for this notion of the moral efficacy of biography in Plutarch's prefatory declaration in his *Life of Pericles* that he persevered with his biographical writings through conviction that the virtuous example of the actions of good men could stimulate imitation by his audience.[5] At the same time as Paschal reproduced this commonplace of biographical writing, however, he also offered an intriguing variation on traditional notions of the function of exemplarity. Paschal transcended the conception of biographically mediated imitation as being an exclusive affair between the reader and the subject of the biography, one that did not implicate the biographer, except as a kind of facilitator. As Paschal piously described his relationship with his subject Pibrac: 'Huius ego viri ut fui primo sectator, mox admirator, ita nunc, quatenque licet, velim esse imitator' ('Guy du Faur de Pibrac, lequel comme je commençai premierement à cognoistre, aussitost je l'admiray, et, maintenant, s'il m'estoit loisible, je le voudrois pouvoir imiter').[6] According to Paschal, it was his personal desire to imitate Pibrac's life that prompted him to compose the biography. Here, too, Plutarch provided a precedent for Paschal's statement. In Plutarch's *Life of Timoleon*, he confessed to the reader that, when he began the project of the *Lives*, he did so for the purpose of inculcating virtue in others, just as he indicated in the *Pericles* preface. As he continued to write the *Lives*, however, he found that his own pleasure in the task spurred him on. Writing biography allowed Plutarch to 'treat history as a mirror'. This in turn enabled him to adorn his own life by imitating the virtues of the men whose actions he described.[7]

Both Paschal and Plutarch, then, shared the ambition of imitating their subjects' actions and moral characters. But Paschal takes the discussion of biographical imitation beyond the Plutarchan model. Unlike his ancient predecessor, Paschal invited the reader of the *Vita*, in the first instance Pierre Forget, to judge his success in fulfilling this aim by contemplating the example of the biographer's own life:

> Utinam quam studiose tam feliciter. Hoc mei, uti spero, mores ostendent. Illud ex aliqua parte indicabit hoc, quicquid est curæ. Nam pietas meum silentium rupit, adeoque verecundiam meam vicit [...]

> Je souhaitterois pour moy y pouvoir rencontrer aussi heureusement comme je m'y estudierois soigneusement, et comme j'espère on le recognoistra par ma vie; tousjours au moins fera-t'on jugement du désir que j'en aurois par ce tesmoignage que j'en rends, quoyque ce soit peu de chose; car la piété a rompu mon silence et a assez eu de pouvoir sur ma modestie [...].[8]

Paschal thus temporarily deflects the reader's gaze from Pibrac's life to his own. Setting modesty aside, he published the life of Pibrac because he wished to position himself deliberately in the line of sight of individuals, like Forget, who held the power to complete his transformation into a second Pibrac, at least at the level of career. By helping Paschal obtain positions in government like those Pibrac had occupied, Forget could accentuate the similarities between the two men's careers. Thus Paschal used his preface to foreground his own imitation of Pibrac.[9] By declaring both his admiration for Pibrac and his own desire to imitate him, Paschal placed himself in the position usually occupied by the reader of a biography.

As for the efficacy of this strategy, Paschal emerged from both the death of Pibrac and that of Henri III, five years later, with his career prospects undimmed. The diplomat Paschal successfully made the transition to the reign of Henri IV (1589–1610). His next important appointment, after that of extraordinary ambassador to Poland in 1576, came in 1589, when he served once again as extraordinary ambassador, this time to England.[10] Paschal's diplomatic career peaked in 1604, when he became resident ambassador to the smaller eastern league of the Rhaetian Alps at Chur in the Grisons (Graubünden), where he remained for a period of ten years. Here, his responsibilities were clearly defined and straightforward enough: to raise men for the French army, to pay them and to prevent enemies of France from hiring Swiss mercenaries. The French resident ambassador to the Grisons also had to report on any troop movement through the Alpine passes.[11] This appointment seems to have been admirably suited to Paschal's temperament. During the sojourn in Switzerland, he had enough time on his hands to pursue his study of ancient authors and to compose an impressively erudite antiquarian work on crowns in the ancient world.[12]

In between 1589 and his Swiss appointment in 1604, Paschal continued to rise in the royal administration. He followed a career path which bears comparison with that of Pibrac, even if it charted a slightly less elevated course. In 1592, at the age of forty-five, Paschal was appointed 'avocat général' at the *parlement* of Rouen. Pibrac had also been a magistrate in a provincial *parlement*: in his native Toulouse. However, Pibrac had become 'avocat général du roi' at the *parlement* of Paris by the time he was thirty-six, on the nomination of Michel de L'Hospital (1505–73). As for Paschal, he did not fulfill his functions as 'avocat général' at Rouen for very long. Rouen, which had declared in favour of the Duc de Mayenne's Catholic *Ligue*, was besieged by Henri IV from 1590 to 1592, and recognized royal authority only in 1594. During the uprising of the *Ligue*, Henri IV appointed Paschal to help restore order to the provinces of Languedoc, Provence, and Dauphiné, which refused to recognize royal authority. In 1578, Pibrac had joined Catherine de Médicis on a similar journey to Languedoc and Guyenne as she attempted to pacify the south.[13] Both men were rewarded for their service to their monarchs by their nomination as 'conseillers d'Etat'. Paschal's Swiss embassy interrupted his period of service on the council. Upon his return to Paris from the Grisons in 1614, however, he took up his post again. An attack of paralysis finally compelled him to retire to his château de Quente near Abbeville, where he died at nearly eighty years old in 1625. Thus Pibrac's career had provided a template for that of Paschal, whose success directly correlates to his ability to follow a career pattern established by his patron.

Truth and Lies in Diplomacy and Biography

That Pibrac's career might seem worth imitating in every respect also owes much to Paschal's biographical art. As we have seen, in Paschal's dedication of the *Vita*, he hinted loudly at his own ambition to imitate the model he depicted in Pibrac. In the body of the biography, he proceeded to demonstrate his ability to imitate Pibrac as an ambassador, accomplishing this by crafting a diplomatic life narrative of Pibrac. While it generally manages to avoid outright lies, the biography certainly neglects to illuminate fully the dubious episodes in Pibrac's career, such as his conduct in the aftermath of the St. Bartholomew's Day Massacre (23–24 August 1572) when he acted as apologist for Henri d'Anjou. D'Anjou, then a candidate for the Polish throne, was widely considered to be one of the instigators of the massacre. In the *Letter to Elvidius*, written by Pibrac but published anonymously to justify the actions of the French monarchy towards a European audience, the author displayed an apparent nonchalance about the loss of life in the events of 23–24 August 1572: 'I am well aware that there were a few murders, but what of it? In such a great disorder, it is impossible to act otherwise.'[14] The callous sentiments expressed here are unlikely to be Pibrac's own, as his desire to avoid bloodshed is a matter of historical record. On 26 August 1572, Charles IX held a 'lit de justice' at which Pibrac demanded before the assembled *parlement* that the king put an immediate end to the violence that was quickly spreading from Paris to the provinces. In the *Letter to Elvidius*, however, Pibrac represented the order to halt the killing as coming entirely from the king himself. In actual fact, on 24 or 25 August, Charles had given orders to conduct massacres outside of Paris, and only on 30 August did he change his policy and command that the violence cease.[15] Paschal, in the *Vita*, could not record Pibrac's earlier demand for a halt to the killings without besmirching Charles's behaviour, something clearly not in the interests of one seeking a career in royal administration. Likewise, Paschal could not account for Pibrac's manipulation of the truth in the *Letter to Elvidius* without seriously undermining his portrait of him as a man of perfect integrity. As Paschal repeatedly insisted in the *Vita*, Pibrac's thoughts and his words, in both speech and writing, never diverged from one another.[16] Paschal therefore decided not to mention either the massacre or the *Letter to Elvidius* in his biography. Still, Paschal evidently felt the need to defend Pibrac indirectly against the possible charge of condoning the massacre, since elsewhere in the biography, he dwelt on Pibrac's horror of bloodshed.[17]

In the *Vita*, Paschal likewise maintained a discreet silence about Pibrac's tempestuous relationship with the young queen of Navarre, Marguerite de Valois (1553–1615), whom he had served as chancellor towards the end of his life and for whom he was widely suspected of harbouring a 'passion extrême'. In August 1578, Pibrac had replaced his brother Louis as chancellor in the households of both Henri de Navarre and his wife.[18] By 1580, however, Marguerite quarrelled with Pibrac, against whom she levelled a number of contradictory accusations. In particular, Marguerite charged Pibrac with attempting to further sabotage her already difficult relations with both her brother, Henri III, and her husband. She suspected Pibrac of trying to orchestrate her movements to ensure his own return to Paris, where he had business as president of the *parlement* as well as being councillor to the king.[19] In addition, Marguerite charged Pibrac with financial mismanagement and with enriching himself at her expense in the sale of her Paris residence which he bought from her and then resold at a tidy profit. Finally, Marguerite was offended by Pibrac's epistolary declaration of his passion for her. Pleading ill health, Pibrac declined to respond immediately to all of Marguerite's accusations but declared himself ready to slit his own throat, if, on further consideration, he recognized a single one of her allegations to be true.[20] Unmoved, Marguerite asked for the return of her seals on 25 September 1581.

As with the *Letter to Elvidius*, Pibrac's passion for the beautiful young queen (whether or not it existed in reality), was a matter of common knowledge and public record. Pibrac apparently confided his love for Marguerite to his friend, the historian Jacques-Auguste de Thou, who duly chronicled it in his *Mémoires*.[21] What is worse, Marguerite showed her husband Pibrac's letters, thus exposing him to public ridicule from satirists and gossip-mongers.[22] Verses composed during Pibrac's lifetime mock him for leaving his post as president of the Paris *parlement* to be near his beloved Marguerite.[23] Pibrac had justified his conduct to Marguerite in a lengthy manuscript *Apologie* which he spent one year painstakingly composing and which was certainly designed for circulation.[24] Responding to Marguerite's specific charge of his declaration of love for her, Pibrac blamed stylistic convention: 'notre façon d'escrire aujourd'huy en France est pleine d'excès et de toute extrémité [...]'.[25]

For his part, Paschal simply chose not to mention the affair rather than to confront the scandal directly. Pibrac's appointment as Marguerite's chancellor receives only a parenthetical mention in Paschal's biography.[26] Curiously, though, Paschal does write about Pibrac's final illness, which dates from the same year as his quarrel with Marguerite, in terms which are highly suggestive of one suffering from a broken heart:

> Nemo illum quatuor ferme ab hinc annis convenit, cui is perpetua quadam sollicitudine non videretur ægrescere. Cui ægritudini ipse, pro virili portione, remedia conquirebat non vulgaria [...] mox enim ad serias cogitationes idemtidem recurrens, libertatem, et secretum dolori suo, et in interna moestitia, pene dixerim, voluptatem quærebat.

> Quelques quatre ans auparavant qu'il mourust, on ne le veid jamais que triste et affligé d'un soing continuel qui le rongeoit. Il faisoit tout ce qui lui estoit possible pour se désennuyer, ne se servant pas de remèdes communs [...] car

> aussitost, retournant à ses ordinaires et plus sérieuses pensées, il recherchoit la solitude pour se douloir en liberté, comme y trouvant quelque sorte de volupté en ses angoisses secrettes et intérieures.[27]

Paschal openly attributed Pibrac's suffering to his love of his country, wracked by religious strife and violence.[28] Still, to an informed reader, Paschal's description of how Pibrac vainly attempted to seek consolation in his official duties gives the impression of a man in the grips of love-sickness. Pibrac's behaviour recalls that of the conventional Petrarchan lover, who wanders the deserted fields 'solo e pensoso'.[29]

Thus, Paschal's attitude towards his biographical subject remains unambiguously idealizing. His Pibrac could be counted on to behave as a virtuous magistrate who demonstrated prudence and sober moderation in the most morally testing of circumstances. In creating a portrait of Pibrac as so entirely blameless, Paschal reveals his gratitude to his patron. However, in his whitewashing of certain episodes from Pibrac's career, Paschal not only acted as a grateful client, but also conformed to his own prescriptions for the way the perfect ambassador should behave with respect to the truth. Truth and lies in diplomacy form the topic of chapter 54 of his handbook for envoys, the *Legatus*. Here, Paschal starts by extolling the virtue of truth-telling in the perfect ambassador. The perfect ambassador should 'shine by the truth, the best assured of virtues'. However, he adds: 'But I am not so boorishly exacting as to entirely close the lips of the envoy to efficacious lies'.[30] So long as the ambassador's underlying intent was honest, Paschal allowed him a certain creative licence with the truth. This advice to diplomats also served Paschal well as a representational strategy in the *Vita*: Pibrac figures as an exemplar of virtue, and his biographer as an able diplomat-in-waiting.

Paschal's Portrait of the Ideal Ambassador

In what follows, I should like to draw out some of the similarities between Paschal's representation of Pibrac in the *Vita* and the portrait of the model ambassador which emerges both from contemporary treatises on the art of diplomacy and from Paschal's own subsequent *Legatus*. These similarities emerge when we consider how Paschal treats the conventional topics or commonplaces of biography. The specifics of his discussion of Pibrac's life relate closely to the nine conventional topics of invention (*loci inventionis*) of epideictic rhetoric regularly transmitted in handbooks of rhetoric: *patria* ('native land'), *maiores* ('ancestors'), *patres* ('parents'), *genesis* ('birth'), *natura* ('character'), *educatio* ('education'), *virtutes* ('virtues'), *facta* or *res gestæ* ('deeds'), and finally, *finis hominis* ('manner of death').[31] Reflecting on these categories helped the orator or writer to generate the material for composition. In the dedication of the *Vita*, Paschal followed ancient biographical commonplace in comparing his textual representation of Pibrac to graphic portraiture in the form of sculpture, engraving or painting. Because of his lack of skill in these arts, Paschal could only hope to present to his dedicatee an imitation of Pibrac's inner soul rather than an exact depiction of his physical appearance:

> Si statuarius essem, cœlator, aut pictor, oris effigiem ære ducerim, cælamine excuderem, coloribus delinearem. Id quando præstare non valeo, divinum animum quo possum effigiatu tibi spectandum præbeo.
>
> Si j'estois sculpteur ou statuaire, ou quelque excellent peintre, je graverois dans le cuivre ou relèverois en bronze les traicts et la majesté de son visage, et y donnerois les couleurs et les ombres, n'oubliant rien de l'art de la peinture; mais n'estant pas ma profession, je me contenteray de vous faire veoir par ce crayon que je vous en tireray, au mieux qu'il me sera possible, l'effigie de son divin esprit.[32]

Just as portraitists in the sixteenth century tended to conform to an iconographic precedent, though, so too did Paschal imitate a recognizable type in his characterization of Pibrac.[33]

In the *Vita*, Paschal concerned himself principally with the art and practice of diplomacy. Paschal placed Pibrac's own experience as a diplomat — first as Charles IX's lay ambassador to the Council of Trent in 1562, and later as member of Henri d'Anjou's entourage on his election as king of Poland in 1573 — at the centre of his biography. A dramatic narrative account of the Polish mission occupies a far greater place in the biography than any of Pibrac's activities in France. But it was not only by focusing on his diplomatic service that Paschal identified Pibrac as belonging to the type of perfect ambassador. In addition, Paschal's described Pibrac's family background, education, talents, moral character and physical aspect, aspects which strongly call to mind the contents of sixteenth-century treatises dealing with the identity of the ideal ambassador, such as those by Gentili or Maggi and indeed, they foreshadow Paschal's own *Legatus*.

Paschal would have been intimately familiar with these treatises, all of which contained strikingly similar recommendations. Books on this topic had begun to proliferate in the mid-sixteenth century in both Italy and France as diplomatic service became an important part of the courtier's career.[34] Paschal's own contribution to the genre, the *Legatus*, appeared some fifteen years after the publication of the *Vita Pibrachii*. To judge by the numerous editions of this 400-odd page tome from its first appearance in Rouen in 1598 to the 1640s, it was required reading for diplomats in the early seventeenth century. Shortly after the first publication of the *Legatus*, Henri IV appointed Paschal to serve as his ambassador to the Swiss canton of Grisons. Paschal went on to publish his own chronicle of the events which occurred during this diplomatic mission in the *Legatio rhetica*.[35] Both the *Legatio rhetica* and the *Legatus* show a good deal of reflection on the theory and practice of diplomacy. It is certainly tempting to view both the *Legatus*, and the *Vie de Pibrac*, as instrumental in securing Paschal's diplomatic appointment to the Grisons. At the time of writing the *Vie de Pibrac*, Paschal had himself of course already served as an ambassador on a mission to Poland. Drawing attention to Pibrac's adventures as a diplomat in Poland would indirectly have recalled Paschal's own accomplishments there.

Treatises on the ideal ambassador, along with Paschal's own *Legatus*, thus constitute an intriguing interpretative key to the portrait of Pibrac. Like that of Gentili before him, Paschal's definition of the ambassador, in the first chapter of the *Legatus*, cites eloquence and intellect as central to the diplomatic role.[36] Paschal argued grandiloquently, and optimistically, that, provided the ambassador was a persuasive orator, external oppression could be broken, anger mollified, hatred defused, and clemency obtained.[37] In the *Pibrachii Vita*, Pibrac perfectly illustrated Paschal's definition of the ideal ambassador with his combination of eloquence and intellect. Although he frequently encountered threatening situations, he never once resorted to taking up arms to resolve conflicts.

Like most writers on diplomacy in this period, Paschal adduced Mercury as the tutelary deity of the ambassador.[38] Paschal included a chapter in the *Legatus* discussing the official symbols ambassadors in the ancient world carried to identify them. This chapter begins with a learned disquisition on Mercury's traditional attribute, the caduceus, and its significance.[39] That Mercury also put in a cameo appearance in the *Vie de Pibrac* further supports the association between Pibrac and the model ambassador. Paschal's reference to Pibrac as 'alter Mercurius caduceum ferens' ('un autre Mercure, portant son caducée en main') transcends pure rhetorical ornamentation to signify his diplomatic identity.[40]

Although the *Legatus* contains its fair share of antiquarian erudition, it also served as a practical work of reference for the contemporary diplomat. And Paschal, again taking his cue from predecessors such as Gentili, anchored firmly in the cultural context of the late sixteenth century the chapter he devoted to the appropriate social background of the ambassador. As all theoreticians of the ideal ambassador concurred, he should be a man of property from a good family.[41] In selecting an ambassador for a particular mission, Paschal proposed as a general rule that the more glorious his family name, the more challenging his mandate should be.[42] Paschal made clear in the *Legatus* that he did not set fortune over virtue in his insistence on pedigree. Rather, he considered that ancestral wealth betokened the gentleman's upbringing necessary for the role. Pibrac exemplified Paschal's views on the social background of the perfect ambassador: his ancestors possessed both pedigree and virtue. In the *Vita*, Paschal supplied Pibrac with a lengthy genealogy, pausing in particular over his ancestor Gratian du Faur, whom Louis IX sent as his ambassador to the court of the Holy Roman Emperor.[43] Paschal also granted considerable space in the biography to Pibrac's father. Responsible for his son's early education, the elder Pibrac saw to it that the boy had teachers who could instruct him — in a turn of phrase worthy of Montaigne — 'non garrire, aut disputare, sed vivere' ('non pas à parler simplement, mais à bien vivre').[44]

An early training in ethics, such as that Pibrac received from his father, was important for the ideal ambassador, who needed to have a solid moral core, and a well-regulated family life. His own moral integrity would in turn allow him to see to the morality of all the others accompanying him on his mission. Paschal could not risk contaminating his portrait of the ambassador by association with the secret agent or intriguer. After all, the diplomat and the spy were not always so readily distinguishable and the corruptible ambassador might all too easily find himself entangled in conspiracy, intrigue and bluff.[45] Paschal would have wished to banish any hint of such sedition, corruption and intrigue from his portrait of Pibrac as the perfect ambassador. Hence he trumpeted Pibrac's moral integrity at every opportunity. Paschal's Pibrac possessed impeccable morals which earned him the accolade of being a sovereign observer and censor of the morals of his day.[46] As for family life, although Paschal made no mention of Pibrac's wife, he did refer to his beloved eldest son, whose death the *Plaisirs de la vie rustique* lament. Outside of his family circle, Pibrac chose his friends not for personal gain, but out of love of virtue.[47]

In common with other contemporary writers on the model ambassador, Paschal treated the question of his education. On the ambassador's education, we find a significant shift in focus from treatises written around the mid-sixteenth century and later works, contemporaneous with the *Vita*.[48] Earlier authors, such as Maggi, wished the ambassador to possess an extremely high level of culture, and to be universally educated in subjects ranging from draughtsmanship and music to logic and mathematics.[49] His competence in the more frivolous of these areas would guarantee his mobility within court circles and his ability to garner the sympathy of the European nobility. Being well liked at court would in turn help to ensure the success of his mission. By the time Paschal was writing, however, the ideal of encyclopaedic culture had faded in favour of more circumscribed, professionally 'useful' forms of learning, in particular, history, jurisprudence and moral philosophy. For Gentili, the ambassador should follow a curriculum that blended history with moral and political philosophy, forming practical guides to his conduct. Gentili did not require any study of natural philosophy, since men of action did not need to indulge in vain speculation about celestial phenomena or the ebb and flow of tides.[50] Although Paschal stipulated that the ambassador should have a general knowledge of human affairs, the *Legatus* specifies that the ideal ambassador should have particular expertise in the disciplines of law and history, both foreign and domestic.[51] Moreover, in terms of moral philosophy, Paschal affirmed that the ambassador should be distinguished by his capacity to employ reason, which divinely illuminates the human mind and permits the accurate judgement of right and wrong action.[52]

Paschal's description of Pibrac's education certainly follows the curriculum set out for the ideal ambassador. In educating his young son, Pibrac's father was, as we have seen, keen that he learn how to live a morally upright life, and not just how to speak correctly. Thus the elder Pibrac selected his son's tutors for their virtue and piety.[53] In a passage which recalls Montaigne's writings on pedagogy, Paschal poured scorn on the kind of useless learning which passed for education in the colleges. He castigated:

> [...] istos [...] literatores, qui adulescentulorum imperitiæ sueti, sibi tergeminum sophos mugire videntur, si ea docuerint, quæ, si scires, dediscenda essent [...]

> [...] ces pédans lesquels, abusans de la simplicité de ceste jeunesse, s'imaginent estre de grands personnages et avoir toute la science en leur cervelle, quand ils leur enseignent des choses que, si vous les sçaviez, vous seriez par après en peine de les désapprendre.[54]

As a student in Paris, Pibrac considered that man's earthly happiness and contentment came from a solid grounding in philosophy, which one should honour as the fount of all knowledge.[55] In later years, Pibrac favoured the moralist Seneca amongst philosophers.[56] After recognizing the importance of philosophy, Pibrac then turned to the study of law, not as a compendium of rules and regulations, but as the foundation for human society.[57] Thoroughly versed in both Latin and Greek, Pibrac garnered a reputation for eloquence. He then proceeded to make a thorough study of ancient and modern history. Although his reading was chronological and careful, Pibrac used his knowledge of history to form his own judgements about human behaviour rather than to stockpile irrelevant details in his memory.[58] In sum, his education helped him first to regulate his own ethical behaviour and later to serve the public good.[59] Like that of the ideal ambassador, Pibrac's education, clearly oriented towards public service, had a pragmatic bent to it.

As far as literary studies were concerned, the theorists conceded that, though the ambassador need not pursue them zealously, he might, with certain caveats, find poetry useful. While excessive bookishness was certainly deleterious to the ambassador's mission, occasional forays into elegant versification might serve him well both as an adornment to his character, and potentially also as an instrument of fame.[60] Paschal's account of Pibrac's activities as a poet accords very definitely with this model. Pibrac's interest in poetry manifested itself early on and his first verses were pleasing to the ear, without being: 'ut ait Catullus, *Molliculi, ac parum pudici*' ('comme dit Catulle: "Lascifs et peu honnestes"').[61] This talent for poetry was just one of the qualities by which Pibrac won a reputation, both at home and abroad — undeniably useful for a future ambassador. Later on, while accompanying Henri d'Anjou through Germany and Italy back to France for his coronation, Pibrac composed his *Quatrains* — 126 poems containing 'preceptes et enseignements utiles pour la vie de l'homme' destined to be highly influential in the seventeenth century.[62] Paschal presented Pibrac's writing as compatible with his office: 'tamen is in mediis prope turbis secretum inveniens, atque ita propemodum ac si inter nemora ipsa, et lucos versaretur, Musarum se choro immiscuit' ('toutesfois il avoit cela de propre que, trouvant tousjours (je ne sçay comment) quelque lieu retiré au beau milieu de la foule, il carressoit les Muses tout ainsi que s'il eust esté dans les bois à l'escart'.[63] Useful to others, Pibrac's neo-Stoic quatrains testified to his good moral character.

Most theoreticians of diplomacy agreed that the model ambassador should possess the ability to adapt to rapidly changing circumstances and to think (and speak) on his feet. As Juan Antonio de Vera y Figueroa would later observe, the perfect ambassador must travel alone to foreign countries where he would frequently need to deal with unforeseen matters. On such occasions, the ambassador's most trusted companion should be his intellect ('esprit'), which he must take good care to keep both sharp and supple, ensuring his ability to react quickly to shifts in circumstance.[64] Similarly, Alberico Gentili insisted on the ambassador's 'ingenium'.[65] By 'ingenium', Gentili referred not simply to the ambassador's capacity for 'bon mots' or witty repartee, but to the sort of quick thinking and inventiveness needed to confront the unpredictable. Paschal praised Pibrac for precisely this kind of intellectual dexterity.[66] Paschal's narrative of events in Poland also emphasized the element of surprise, giving Pibrac ample opportunity to display this particular virtue. When qualifying the kind of eloquence he desired in his model ambassador, Paschal wrote in the *Legatus* that his speech should be ready ('promptus') and flowing ('profluens').[67] In the *Vie de Pibrac*, Paschal specifically praised Pibrac's eloquence for its astounding facility. Remarkably at ease when he extemporized, Pibrac readily adapted his speech to any possible subject or situation, of whatever order of magnitude, all the while managing to preserve perfect Latinity.[68]

Renaissance writers on the ideal ambassador concurred that, in addition to being of good moral character and sound intellect, he should also possess an attractive appearance.[69] Paschal likewise devoted a chapter of the *Legatus* to the ambassador's external aspect.[70] As with the question of the ambassador's family background, Paschal sought not to ascribe too much importance to qualities within the sole purview of fortune. Always the pragmatist, though, Paschal was prepared to grasp advantage wherever it lay. Thus he declared that, although fortune neither directed nor helped in the cultivation of virtue, this was no reason to contemn her bounty.[71] Furthermore, Paschal decreed, inner virtue often suffused the body's surface with a glow, like a divine light, as the beautiful soul enriched its dwelling place.[72] Paschal catalogued at some length examples of various physical flaws which, in his view, rendered a man unsuitable for appointment as an ambassador by making him a potential subject of mockery. These ranged in severity from conditions which hindered mobility, such as mutilated or withered limbs, and a hunchback, to defects which merely detracted from canonical beauty, like a broken nose, facial blemishes or baldness.

After carefully detailing those physical qualities unacceptable in an ambassador, Paschal logically proceeded to give an account of desirable features. Compared to the graphic description of defects, the treatment of how the ideal ambassador should look noticeably lacks visual specificity:

> [...] how pleasant it is to behold a calm and earnest face, a gentle step, a modest bearing, in short, a man whose whole outward appearance is worthy of honour ('venerabilem'). So far as anyone examines such a man, he may easily infer that he is a good man, and believe him to be frank and vigorous.[73]

Likewise, in the *Vita*, Paschal did not provide a detailed physical description of Pibrac.[74] The scattered references to Pibrac's appearance or to the impression his external aspect has on others are as vague as his portrait of the ideal ambassador from the *Legatus* cited above. For example, in 1548, aged just nineteen, Pibrac had recently returned from Italy. When recounting his Italian travels, he did so soberly, with an earnest gravity, speaking like a much older man, such that his intellectual maturity contrasted with the youthfulness of his visage.[75] Paschal referred repeatedly to Pibrac's extraordinary modesty which rendered him both commendable and loveable.[76] The calm, gently composed self-assurance of Paschal's ideal ambassador is also in keeping with another quality Paschal attributed to Pibrac, that of gentleness.[77] While Paschal's model ambassador should be quiet and unobtrusive — as appropriate for one whose office it is to represent another, speaking not for himself but for his king — his submissiveness never reaches the point of servility. The perfect ambassador was frank and vigorous, in other words, a nobleman with an aristocratic conception of his own freedom and dignity. Pibrac showed just this kind of robustness. He displayed a bold magnanimity at the reception held for Henri d'Anjou on his arrival in Poland in 1574 and, later, addressed the Polish senate with a self-assured resolve.[78] When a band of brigands attacked Pibrac on his return to Poland in April 1575, he miraculously won over their captain. This man went from being the brigand most resolved in favour of executing Pibrac to become his most fervent defender. The reason for his change of heart lay in Pibrac's appearance: his gentle speech and imposingly majestic countenance.[79] Once freed, Pibrac did not give in to a display of passionate anger. Rather, he continued to radiate his customary gracious serenity.[80]

In addition to being attractive in his person and affecting a calm composure when he confronted other dignitaries on public business, Paschal's ideal ambassador must also be physically strong with good endurance.[81] This was needful for one who spent much of his time on his feet at court, either standing in attendance or walking about.[82] Paschal also imagined the possibility that the ambassador might, on occasion, literally need to get his feet wet, encountering greater adversity than the normal discomforts of court life. To illustrate this point, Paschal provided several examples of ambassadors who, in times of war when no other reliable transport was available, swam heroically across rivers to carry out their missions.[83] Pibrac clearly fulfilled this requirement, as demonstrated by the high point of Paschal's biography: Pibrac's daring escape from Poland after Henri d'Anjou fled his responsibilities as Polish king to take up the French throne. On this perilous journey, Pibrac notably had to cross a rapidly flowing river with little more than a tree branch as a precarious flotation device.[84]

To conclude, then: my reading of Paschal's *Life of Pibrac* suggests that it provided its author with a useful means to script his own career in the royal administration. Paschal, as a young man, relatively new to court, was — like Budé's biographer, Le Roy — in need of forging his own reputation and of securing reliable channels of patronage. By inscribing himself in his biography of a leading figure at court, he was able to intimate his own suitability to follow in Pibrac's traces. His explicit presentation of Pibrac as a model for imitation by the reader might seem at first to belong to the rhetorical conventions of ancient biography inherited, for example, from Plutarch; moreover, the kinds of information he furnishes about Pibrac's life relate closely to the conventional topics (*loci*) of epideictic rhetoric transmitted in most handbooks of rhetoric. Paschal innovated, however, in several key ways. First, in the preface, he does more than simply draw attention to his own desire to imitate Pibrac — Plutarch had already done this in his *Life of Timoleon* — but he encourages his potential patron to judge for himself the biographer's success in being like Pibrac. To facilitate the identification of the two men, Paschal fashioned Pibrac largely in his own image by his second key biographical innovation. Paschal's treatment of the *loci* of *inventio* imbues his portrait of Pibrac with the chief characteristics of the model Renaissance diplomat. By focusing the biography on Pibrac's ambassadorial career, Paschal cleverly managed to keep alive the memory of his success in his first diplomatic mission in 1576. First, Paschal displayed his aptitude for judicious presentation of the truth, adopting a 'diplomatic' representational strategy that omitted some of the morally dubious episodes in Pibrac's career. Then, by magnifying the resemblances between Pibrac and the exemplary diplomat, depicted in contemporary treatises on the art of diplomacy, Paschal highlighted those qualities he would like to be identified as possessing and which might help to secure his appointment on future diplomatic missions. Paschal's nomination, some twenty years after he published the biography of Pibrac, to the desirable post of resident ambassador at Grisons vindicated his representational strategy.

Notes to Chapter 2

1. *Vidi Fabricii Pibrachii Vita, scriptore Carolo Paschalio...* (Paris: Robert Colombel, 1584). A descendent of Pibrac's, Guy du Faur de Hermay, published a French translation in 1617: *La Vie et mœurs de messire Guy du Faur, seigneur de Pybrac...* (Paris: Thibault du Val). Further citations of the *Vie de Pibrac* are from the text in Cimber and Danjou, *Archives curieuses de l'histoire de France*, 1st series, 15 vols (Paris: Beauvais, 1834–37), x (1836), pp. 219–97.
2. Roman d'Amat, *Dictionnaire de biographie française*, fasc. 80 (Paris: Letouzey & Ané, 1976), pp. 479–82. Michaud & Michaud, *Biographie universelle ancienne et moderne*, 45 vols (Paris: Desplaces, 1854–65), xiv (1856), 397.
3. Hampton, *Writing from History*, pp. ix–x.
4. *C. Cornelii Taciti ... ab excessu Divi Augusti Annalium libri quatuor priores, et in hos observationes C. Paschalii* (Paris: Robert Colombel, 1581). See Arnaldo Momigliano, 'The first political commentary on Tacitus', in *Contributo alla storia degli studi classici*, Storia e letteratura. Raccolta di studi e testi, 47 (Rome: Edizioni di Storia e Letteratura, 1955), pp. 37–59; Peter Burke, 'Tacitism', in *Tacitus*, ed. by T. A. Dorey (London: Routledge & Kegan Paul, 1969), pp. 149–71 (p. 150).
5. Plutarch, 'Pericles', pp. 165–67.
6. *Pibrachii Vita*, fol. 2v°; *Vie de Pibrac*, p. 222.
7. Plutarch, 'Life of Timoleon', in *The Age of Alexander*, trans. Ian Scott-Kilvert (Harmondsworth: Penguin, 1973), pp. 151–52.
8. *Pibrachii Vita*, fol. 3; *Vie de Pibrac*, pp. 222–23.
9. Only in the French translation is the expected invitation to imitation eventually extended to the reader of the *Pibrachii Vita* as well, almost as an afterthought: 'Pour prendre un bon et sage conseil il faut regarder dans le miroir de sa prudence; pour une intégrité de vie il se faut proposer ses mœurs et façons de faire, en quoy il n'y avoit rien à désirer; en un mot, toute sa vie doit estre un modelle et patron sur lequel on doit former la sienne' (*Vie de Pibrac*, p. 222). The Latin focuses exclusively on the biographer's imitation of his subject: 'In illius prudentiæ speculum intueor, ad consilium mores deligo ad integritatem; totam vitam mihi propono, ut exemplum' (*Pibrachii Vita*, fols. 2v°–3r°).
10. Momigliano, 'The first political commentary', p. 50.
11. Garrett Mattingly, *Renaissance Diplomacy* (London: Cape, 1955), p. 174.
12. *Coronæ, opus decem librum distinctum* (Paris: A. Perier, 1610).
13. Robert J. Knecht, *Catherine de' Medici* (London: Longman, 1998), pp. 193–201.
14. 'Animadversum in paucos scio, sed quid agas? In tanto tumultu aliter fieri non posse, nec expedire'. *L'Apologie de la Saint-Barthélemy par Guy Du Faur de Pibrac*, ed. and trans. by Alain Cabos (Paris: Champion & Cocharaux, 1922), p. 10.
15. Cabos, *Pibrac*, pp. 224–25.
16. *Pibrachii Vita*, fol. 30; *Vie de Pibrac*, pp. 267–68.
17. *Pibrachii Vita*, fol. 41v°; *Vie de Pibrac*, p. 288.
18. Loris Petris, 'Chronologie', in Guy du Faur de Pibrac, *Les Quatrains*, ed. by Loris Petris (Geneva: Droz, 2004), p. 6.
19. Marguerite de Valois, *Mémoires et autres écrites. 1574–1614*, ed. by Eliane Viennot (Paris: H. Champion, 1999), pp. 197–98. See Jules Claretie, 'Notice', in Guy du Faur de Pibrac, *Les Quatrains* (Paris: A. Lemerre, 1874 ; repr. Geneva: Slatkine Reprints, 1969), p. 41.
20. Cabos, *Pibrac*, p. 293.
21. Cabos, *Pibrac*, p. 298.
22. Pierre de l'Estoile, *Régistre-Journal du règne de Henri III*, ed. by Madeleine Lazard and Gilbert Schrenck, 6 vols (Geneva: Droz, 1992–2006), iii (1997), p. 175. Pétris, 'Chronologie', p. 6.

23. Claretie, 'Notice', pp. 40–41.
24. 'Apologie de Monsieur de Pybrac à la Royne de Navarre', BNF Coll Dupuy n° 60, Coll des Cinq Cents de Colbert n° 19. The letter, dated 1 October 1581, was sent in Autumn 1582. Cabos, *Pibrac*, p. 298.
25. 'Apologie de Monsieur de Pybrac', cited in Cabos, *Pibrac*, p. 312.
26. *Pibrachii Vita*, fol. 42v°; *Vie de Pibrac*, p. 289.
27. *Pibrachii Vita*, fols. 44–45; *Vie de Pibrac*, pp. 292–94.
28. *Pibrachii Vita*, fol. 43v°; *Vie de Pibrac*, p. 291.
29. Petrarch, *Canzoniere*, 35, v.1. Francesco Petrarca, *Canzoniere. Rerum vulgarium fragmenta*, ed. by Rosanna Bettarini, 2 vols (Turin: Einaudi, 2005) I, 189.
30. 'Non sum tamen ita rustice torvus, ut officiosum mendacium omnino excludam ex ore legati'. Paschal, *Legatus* (Paris: P. Chevalier, 1612), p. 250.
31. The principal sources for epideictic in the Renaissance were the anonymous *Rhetorica ad Herennium* (3.10), preserved together with the rhetorical works of Cicero, Quintilian's *Institutio Oratoria* (3.7), and Aphthonius's *Progymnasmata*, in Rudolph Agricola's Latin translation. See George A. Kennedy, *Classical Rhetoric and its Christian and Secular Tradition from Ancient to Modern Times* (London: Croon Helm, 1980), pp. 195–219; and Paul J. Smith, 'Rabelais' *Pantagruel* and *Gargantua* as Mock-Biographies', in *Modelling the Individual: Biography and Portrait in the Renaissance*, ed. by Karl Enenkel, Betsy de Jong-Crane, and Peter Liebregts (Amsterdam and Atlanta, GA: Rodopi, 1998), pp. 153–72.
32. *Pibrachii Vita*, fol. 3; *Vie de Pibrac*, p. 223. See, for example, Plutarch, 'Life of Cimon', in *Rise and Fall of Athens*, p. 143 and 'Life of Alexander', in *Age of Alexander*, p. 252. It is intriguing, in the light of my earlier discussion of Paschal's use of the biography of Pibrac as a template for building his own career, that the French translation should describe the *Vie* as a *crayon*, which Cotgrave (1611) defined not only as a broad outline or rough sketch, but also as an example to be followed: 'Dry painting; or, a painting in, or Picture of, dry colours; also, the Table whereon a Painter mingleth (such) colours; and the first draught, or lineaments of a picture, made with any of them; hence also, a patterne, or example'.
33. Joanna Woodall, 'Introduction: Facing the Subject', in *Portraiture: Facing the Subject*, ed. and intro. by Joanna Woodall (Manchester: Manchester University Press, 1997), p. 2.
34. Mattingly, *Diplomacy*, pp. 211–21.
35. *Legatio rhetica, sive relatio earum qui interdecennium in Rhætia acciderunt ab anno 1602 ad annum 1614* (Paris: P. Chevalier, 1620).
36. Alberico Gentili, *De legationibus libri tres* (London: Thomas Vautrollier, 1585), pp. 158–62; Paschal, *Legatus*, p. 1.
37. *Legatus*, p. 7.
38. *Legatus*, p. 8. Gentili, *De legationibus*, pp. 4–5; p. 8. On Mercury as the god of diplomacy, see Daniel Ménager, *Diplomatie et théologie à la Renaissance* (Paris: Presses universitaires françaises, 2001), p. 86.
39. Chapter 5, 'De caducæo: et legationibus iis quæ signis plura demonstrant quam verbis', *Legatus*, pp. 15–20. See Gentili, *De legationibus*, ch 18, pp. 49–54.
40. *Pibrachii Vita*, fol. 39v°; *Vie de Pibrac*, p. 285.
41. Gentili, *De legationibus*, pp. 155–57. Mattingly, *Diplomacy*, p. 215.
42. *Legatus*, p. 57.
43. *Pibrachii Vita*, fol. 4v°; *Vie de Pibrac*, p. 225.
44. *Pibrachii Vita*, fol. 6v°; *Vie de Pibrac*, p. 228.
45. Mattingly, *Diplomacy*, p. 196.
46. *Pibrachii Vita*, fol. 41; *Vie de Pibrac*, p. 287.
47. *Pibrachii Vita*, fol. 45; *Vie de Pibrac*, p. 294.
48. Mattingly, *Diplomacy*, pp. 216–17. Ménager, *Diplomatie et théologie*, pp. 92–95.
49. Ottaviano Maggi, *De legato libri duo* (Venice: [Ludovico Avanzi?], 1566). Cited in Ménager, *Diplomatie et théologie*, p. 92.
50. Gentili, *De legationibus*, pp. 174–75. Mattingly, *Diplomacy*, p. 217.
51. *Legatus*, p. 61.
52. *Legatus*, p. 61.

53. *Pibrachii Vita*, fol. 6v°; *Vie de Pibrac*, p. 228.
54. *Pibrachii Vita*, fol. 6v°; *Vie de Pibrac*, p. 229. See Montaigne, *Essais*, I, 25 ('Du pédantisme') and 26 ('De l'institution des enfans').
55. *Pibrachii Vita*, fol. 7; *Vie de Pibrac*, p. 229.
56. *Pibrachii Vita*, fol. 44v°; *Vie de Pibrac*, p. 293.
57. *Pibrachii Vita*, fol. 7; *Vie de Pibrac*, p. 230.
58. *Pibrachii Vita*, fol 8v°; *Vie de Pibrac*, p. 232.
59. *Pibrachii Vita*, fol. 8v°; *Vie de Pibrac*, p. 232.
60. Gentili, *De legationibus*, pp. 175–79. Mattingly, *Diplomacy*, p. 217.
61. *Pibrachii Vita*, fol. 8v°; *Vie de Pibrac*, p. 232.
62. *Pibrachii Vita*, fols. 29v°–30; *Vie de Pibrac*, p. 267.
63. *Pibrachii Vita*, fol. 29v°; *Vie de Pibrac*, p. 267.
64. Juan Antonio de Vera y Figueroa, *Le parfait ambassadeur*, trans. by Nicolas Lancelot ([Amsterdam?]: n. publ., 1642) [pirate edn of the first edn, (Paris: A. de Sommaville, 1635)], p. 177. Cited in Ménager, *Diplomatie et théologie*, p. 86.
65. Gentili, *De legationibus*. Cited in Ménager, *Diplomatie et théologie*, p. 95.
66. *Pibrachii Vita*, fol. 12v°; *Vie de Pibrac*, p. 239.
67. *Legatus*, p. 62.
68. *Pibrachii Vita*, fols. 21v°–22; *Vie de Pibrac*, p. 254.
69. Gentili, *De legationibus*, pp. 152–54. Ménager, *Diplomatie et théologie*, p. 87.
70. *Legatus*, ch 16 'Externa desidero in legato', pp. 64–68.
71. *Legatus*, p. 64.
72. *Legatus*, p. 64.
73. 'Contra, quam iuvat tueri faciem tranquillam et seriam, gradum clementem, habitum modestum, denique hominem tota specie venerabilem. Adeo ut quisquis talem aspexerit, bonum virum facile coniiciat, ingenuum ac strenuum libenter credat.' *Legatus*, pp. 66–67.
74. Guy du Faur d'Hermay's 1617 translation does contain a portrait engraving of Pibrac which includes a device taken from Vergil's Georgics (II, 401): 'Labor actus in orbem' (modified from 'redit agricolis labor actus in orbem' [the famer's toil is one long round]).
75. *Pibrachii Vita*, fol. 9v°; *Vie de Pibrac*, p. 234.
76. *Pibrachii Vita*, fols. 12v°, 17v°, 40; *Vie de Pibrac*, p. 240, p. 247, and p. 285.
77. *Pibrachii Vita*, fol. 22; *Vie de Pibrac*, passim, for example, p. 255.
78. *Pibrachii Vita*, fols. 17v°, 27; *Vie de Pibrac*, p. 247 and p. 263.
79. *Pibrachii Vita*, fol. 33v°; *Vie de Pibrac*, p. 273. Compare Paschal's account of Pibrac's liberation with Montaigne's anecdote in 'De la phisionomie' about his own narrow escape from a band of masked attackers during a journey through some dangerous woods. (*Essais*, III.12, pp. 1061–62). Against all expectations, their leader ultimately spares Montaigne. This man subsequently told Montaigne that he owed his freedom to his visage and to his stoic maintenance of a noble composure in both countenance and speech. In this instance, his inner character illuminates his outward appearance with by a kind of divine grace. As Montaigne concludes his narration of this episode: 'Il est possible que la bonté divine se voulut servir de ce vain instrument pour ma conservation' (1062).
80. *Pibrachii Vita*, fol. 34; *Vie de Pibrac*, p. 274.
81. *Legatus*, p. 68.
82. Ménager notes that contemporary theoreticians of diplomacy, concerned about the ambassador's ability to withstand the fatigues of travel between European courts and be able to dance elegantly once he arrived, typically required him to be young (*Diplomatie et théologie*, p. 99).
83. *Legatus*, p. 68.
84. *Pibrachii Vita*, fol. 25v°; *Vie de Pibrac*, p. 261.

Figure 3. Portrait of Ronsard from Jean-Jacques Boissard, *Bibliotheca chalcographica, hoc est virtute et eruditione clarorum virorum imagines* (Heidelberg: Clemens Ammon, 1669), p. 234.

CHAPTER 3

The Traffic of Mercury
Claude Binet and the *Vie de Ronsard* (1586)

At first glance, Claude Binet's *Vie de Ronsard* strikes its reader as a deeply pious text, which attests the biographer's veneration for his subject. As a published poet himself, Binet (1553–1600?) nonetheless remained aware of the unbridgeable distance separating him from the hero of his biography. Binet was content to gaze up at Ronsard with the adoration of a humble disciple. I should like to argue, however, that, on closer scrutiny, Binet's portrayal of Ronsard appears less reverential. The iconic, immutable figure built up by Binet as 'Prince et pere de nos poëtes' yields to a more ambivalent, contingent one. The Ronsard who emerges is, rather like Binet himself, an accomplished courtier, and a writer who is very much the product of his historical circumstances.[1]

Binet's *Vie de Pierre de Ronsard* thus reflects a greater complexity in the relationship between biographer and subject than in the two cases discussed so far. The publishing history of the text is similarly involved. First printed in 1586, the year after Ronsard's death, the *Vie* was the first vernacular biography of a French poet to appear as a separate monograph Life. As such, it proclaims Ronsard's pre-eminent status on the literary scene. In 1587 and again in 1597, Binet produced two substantially revised versions of the *Vie*. These accompanied editions of Ronsard's *Œuvres complètes* which Binet had co-edited. As a result of Binet's revisions, the length of the 1597 text exceeds that of the original by some twenty pages, increased by both rhetorical embellishment on existing material and the inclusion of new anecdotes. Thus Binet's biography belongs to the same process of producing a great-author-figure as the assembling of these *Œuvres complètes* (a work begun by Ronsard himself in 1560), together with the production of commentaries on the two books of the *Amours* by Marc-Antoine de Muret (1526–85) and Remy Belleau (1528?–77).[2]

I should like to begin with an overview of the structure of Binet's biography of Ronsard, as the architecture contributes significantly to shaping our initial perception of Ronsard as a saintly figure. In the rest of this chapter, I shall attempt to problematize a purely hagiographical view of the biography and I shall suggest a number of ways in which Binet used the work in the service of his own glory as well as Ronsard's. In so doing, I shall refer in the first section to the only poem Ronsard dedicated to Binet, the 'Hymne de Mercure'. I shall propose that, as Ronsard's biographer, Binet was operating under the aegis of Mercury. The opportunistic, endlessly inventive behaviour of this deity, as described by Ronsard, provides a convenient model for Binet's transformation of Ronsard's life and poetry into the material of his biography.[3] In this initial section, then, I shall substantiate the association of Binet and Ronsardian Mercury by briefly outlining Binet's variegated career as a poet turned lawyer and magistrate. The second segment of this chapter will analyse three instances from the early part of the *Vie* where Binet uses a poem by Ronsard as the basis for his prose. Binet rewrites Ronsard's verse in ways which advertise his mastery of rhetorical amplification. In the third and final section, I shall discuss two anecdotes Binet added to the 1597 edition of the *Vie*. As I have mentioned, Binet revised his text over a period of ten years. Through this process of revision he invented and reinvented Ronsard to suit the interests of his own self-fashioning. Performing a kind of biographical alchemy, Binet refined his image of Ronsard as a near-divine poet to show him as an ambivalent, mortal being who was a highly skilled courtier — not unlike Binet himself.

So, turning now to the structure of Binet's *Vie de Ronsard*, this resembles a triptych with three distinct sections of roughly equal length. The first segment is a conventional narrative biography which begins with an account of the poet's genealogy and early years. This hagiographical section follows the conventions of conversion narratives. Despite the supernatural signs in his infancy of his future greatness, the adolescent Ronsard began his training as a courtier like any other young boy of his class who was not destined for a military or ecclesiastical career. After a serious illness, a propitious meeting with an initiate of the Muses, and the timely death of his father, Ronsard elected to follow a loftier path and dedicate himself seriously to poetry. Thereafter, while he deployed a strategy of outward accommodation at court, he diligently pursued his real vocation through study and emulation of the ancients.

The second section of the biography depicts Ronsard's final illness and agony. His death during the night of 27 December 1585 represents an apotheosis through poetry. Ronsard remained lucid throughout his excruciating physical decline, composing his *Derniers vers* which he dictated to a devoted Binet. At the same time, he made a confession of faith to his chaplain. The presence of an audience throughout Ronsard's death agony ensured the exemplary value of this spectacle. Binet was as alert to the propaganda value of his text as Ronsard was in the 'Discours des miseres de ce temps', and his overall tone harmonizes well with the emotionalism of counter-Reformation Catholicism. As such, it reads at least in part as a homage to Ronsard's anti-Protestant polemical poetry of the 1560s. Finally, Binet marked Ronsard's passage to the realm of the divine with a detailed account of the pageantry surrounding his funeral service in the chapel of Boncourt.

The third panel of the triptych provides an assessment of Ronsard's literary legacy and includes pronouncements on the current state of French poetry. Binet placed much of this material in Ronsard's own mouth, allowing him to speak from beyond the grave as a divinized poet. A thumbnail sketch of Ronsard's thoroughly noble character and habits — his ready conversation and his love of the gentlemanly pursuits of hunting and gardening — graces this final section of the biography. However, Binet connects all of these seemingly worldly activities very closely with Ronsard's identity as a poet. As the solitary Ronsard strolls on the banks of the Loire, or in the forest of Gastine, he is 'tousjours en la compaignie des Muses'.[4] When in Paris, Ronsard seeks out the bucolic neighbourhoods of Gentilly, Hercueil, or Vanves, not simply for their salubrious freshness, but more importantly because the Muses favour these locations.

Binet's own discreet presence makes itself felt in each of these three sections, like a donor figure at the bottom of the panels of the triptych. The conclusion to the biography affirms its religious atmosphere and thus the hagiography of Ronsard. Here, Binet compares his text to a reliquary urn containing the collected ashes of the dead poet.[5] Consecrating his text with perpetual tears, Binet presents the *Vie* to posterity as evidence of his own and France's devotion to Ronsard. The biography ends with an apostrophe to the dead Ronsard in the language of the invocation of saints. Finally, Binet addresses Ronsard as his spiritual father and prays his soul might rest 'au ciel en toute douceur et paix tranquillement.'

Binet's Career and Ronsard's 'Hymne de Mercure' (1585)

Thus Binet builds the sanctification of Ronsard into the compositional framework of the biography. To gain a different perspective on Binet's activity as a biographer, let us look away from the *Vie de Ronsard* for a moment and consider instead Ronsard's 'Hymne de Mercure'. The one poem certainly dedicated to Binet by Ronsard, it was first published when Binet added it to the 1587 posthumous edition of Ronsard's *Œuvres complètes*.[6] The last of the hymns Ronsard composed, and one of the most innovative, it presents his most extensive and subtle treatment of the god Mercury. It should come as no surprise that Binet proudly mentions this poem and its dedication in his *Vie de Ronsard*.

We find an ostensible explanation for Ronsard's choice of dedicatee at the end of the 'Hymne de Mercure'. In the last lines of the poem, Ronsard evoked the traditional association of Mercury, the messenger god, with eloquence. He flatteringly suggested that Binet's own possession of this quality made him a suitable recipient of the hymn:

> Binet soin d'Apollon, dont la vive eloquence
> Flate mon mal d'espoir, mon procez d'asseurance,
> Au lieu de tes beaux vers, du trafic de nostre art,
> Des honneurs de Mercure icy je te fay part[7]

The 'procez' Ronsard mentioned was his ongoing quarrel with Pierre Guilloré, one of the king's guardsmen, a legal dispute in which Binet was acting on his behalf. By the mid-1580s, the time of this poem's composition, Binet was enjoying a successful career as a lawyer, with a prestigious position as substitute for Jacques de la Guesle as 'procureur général du roi'.[8] Binet had been 'avocat au parlement de Paris' from 1575. His legal career would culminate in his designation in 1587 as 'Lieutenant général de la Sénéchaussée de Riom', an office he obtained through the patronage of Charles IX's widow, Elizabeth of Austria.

In addition to praise for Binet's eloquence as a lawyer, the hymn's conclusion also contains a reference to an exchange of verses between Ronsard and Binet. Ronsard presented his poem to Binet: 'au lieu de tes beaux vers' (v. 201). In the *Vie de Ronsard*, however, Binet would modestly admit his failure to pursue both forms of eloquence, legal and poetic, to the same high standards. Despite the encouragement of so great a poet as Ronsard, Binet confesses that his literary production has been curtailed by conflicting professional demands: 'la sévérité de nos loix'.[9] Such a presentation of the reason for his neglect of the Muses has, of course, the effect of magnifying the importance of his position as a jurist.

And yet, Ronsard's dedication of the 'Hymne de Mercure' to Binet was not an unambiguous tribute to his double eloquence as a lawyer–poet. This is because Ronsard's Mercury is far from being an unequivocally positive figure. As the messenger god, he does indeed possess the quality of eloquence with which he is customarily attributed. However, he also turns out to be the god of theft, imposture and deviousness. Thus Ronsard describes how, at barely three days old, the young god cheekily stole Apollo's cattle. Henceforth, Mercury's father, Jupiter, judges it prudent to oversee his son's education. The educational programme for his son sees him being taught to play the flute by Pan, receiving training in wrestling from the Spartans, and finally, visiting the marketplace. Here, Mercury learns '[...] le trafic et les metiers cachez/ Des marchans pour le gain, artifices, pratiques/ De toutes sortes d'arts pour le gain' (vv. 90–91). As a final stage in his training, Mercury visits an alchemist's laboratory : 'il alla voir fumer/ Les fourneaux qui font l'homme et son bien consommer [...]'. Ronsard's Mercury is a worldly figure, an urban deity, the 'Seigneur des carrefours des places et des rues' (v. 132). He is a mountebank, and an opportunist. Like the element whose name he bears, quicksilver, Mercury can change shape with ease. This elemental association makes Mercury the tutelary deity of invention, who prompts men to devise 'mille mestiers nouveaux' (v. 122).

Ronsard's dedication suggests that these more morally ambivalent, flexible qualities characterized Binet's *modus operandi* as an ambitious courtier under the late Valois, alongside the quality of eloquence, whether deployed as poet or lawyer. As Ullrich Langer has argued, the courtier in the literature of the late sixteenth and early seventeenth centuries emerged as a protean figure, a skilled rhetorician capable of changing his *ethos* — the persuasive appeal of his character — to ensure the continued favour of his prince.[10] Such an unstable figure represented a challenge to the Ciceronian and Aristotelian rhetorical model, which made the four cardinal virtues or *habitus laudabiles* of prudence, justice, strength, and temperance the basis for establishing credibility with one's audience and thus for any eloquent or persuasive speech.[11] The new 'sociable' ethic of court life, by contrast, meant that the courtier should be constantly prepared to assume a novel, even contradictory persona in order to gratify the whims of his prince. As for Binet, he certainly knew how to profit from his circumstances and parlay his literary connections into a series of promotions. Despite his complaints, he managed with exemplary success the transition from aspiring court poet to professional lawyer and prominent magistrate. Like Mercury, who never rests until he has accomplished his aims, Binet consistently demonstrated the ability to reinvent himself in ways which ensured his progress in society. How his connection with Ronsard, and, more specifically, his composition of the *Vie de Ronsard*, facilitated Binet's reinvention of himself and his self-promotion, are questions I should like to address in the remainder of this chapter.

Binet took his first significant step on the path to preferment when he met Ronsard himself. The encounter probably occurred during the latter half of 1570, orchestrated by the scholar–poet Jean Dorat (1508–88), who had taught both men. At this time, Ronsard, after a protracted period of illness spent in his properties in Touraine (1568–69), had returned to Paris to assist Dorat and his friend and secretary Amadis Jamyn with the preparations for the festivities in celebration of the recent marriage between Charles IX and Elizabeth of Austria.[12]

Binet, then just seventeen, had already attracted Dorat's attention as a promising young poet. Dorat presumably hoped that Ronsard would show Binet the ropes at court as well as acting as his poetic mentor. And Binet seems to have proved a most able pupil on both fronts. Binet's first publications demonstrate his ability to exploit favourable circumstances at the Valois court to traffic successfully in verse. The period 1570 to 1575 witnessed intense courtly activity. Charles IX married Elizabeth of Austria at Mézières in November 1570, and the young king entered Paris in March 1571. Ronsard and Dorat, together with the sculptor Germaine Pilon and the painter Niccolò dell'Abate, all collaborated on the elaborate ceremonies for the royal entry. 1572 saw the marriage of Henri de Navarre and Marguerite de Valois, and 1573 Catherine de Médicis's magnificent reception of the Polish ambassadors, who travelled to Paris to greet their newly elected king, Henri d'Anjou (the future Henri III). After Charles's death, in 1574, there were further festivities in February 1575 to mark the marriage of Henri III to Louise de Vaudémont and the new king's own triumphal entry into Paris. In short, an aspiring court poet had ample opportunities to make his mark. Binet recognized this and, by 1573, had published an ode celebrating the birth and baptism of the princess Marie-Isabel, daughter of Charles IX and Elizabeth, as well as two extended poems lamenting the departure of d'Anjou for Poland.

In addition to this encomiastic production, Binet also managed to publish his own *Diverses Poësies* in the same year.[13] Here, he pursued a carefully calibrated strategy that linked him to established poets as a means of guaranteeing a favourable reception for his verse. For instance, Binet included his *Diverses Poësies* in his edition of the poems of Jean de La Péruse, an original member of the Pléiade.[14] A glance at the titles of the poems in Binet's collection makes clear his poetic debt to Ronsard, Dorat and Jamyn: *Sonet pour Jean Dorat à la Santé*; *La Vache de Myron descrite par les Grecs, et depuis par P. de Ronsard*; *Chant forestier ou Le Chasseur au Seigneur Amadis Jamin*. Between 1573 and 1583, Binet regularly contributed to poetic *Tombeaux* as well as composing liminary sonnets, for example, for André Thevet's *Vrais pourtraicts et Vies* (1584). Then, in 1583, Binet published the work for which he is best remembered as a poet: *Les plaisirs de la vie rustique et solitaire*.[15] As its title makes clear, this collection of pastoral poems — then a fashionable genre — took its inspiration from Guy du Faur de Pibrac's *Les plaisirs de la vie rustique*.[16] Binet also dedicated this work to Pibrac, then at the height of his career in government, and it earned him the accolade of a contemporary critic as one of France's best pastoral poets.[17] Once again, Binet had these poems printed along with verses on the same theme by more established figures such as Ronsard and Pibrac.[18] Binet's poetic swan song was the dedication to Henri III of the 1587 edition of Ronsard's *Œuvres complètes*. Here, Binet represented himself in dialogue with the shade of Ronsard about the parlous state of France during a period of civil war. Binet may have borrowed the conceit of a dialogue with the dead poet from Ronsard himself, who spoke with Du Bellay's ghost in his 1560 'Elégie à Loïs Des Masures'.[19]

Thus, in his cunning management of his literary career to ensure maximum visibility, Binet showed similar traits to Mercury whom Ronsard in his 'Hymne de Mercure' described as 'subtil et cauteleux' and well-versed in artful manoeuvring — the 'trafic de finesse'(vv. 95–96). As Ronsard's biographer, Binet was equally susceptible to such trickery, a predisposition which Ronsard's seventeenth-century biographers later recognized. Both Colletet and Bayle attacked Binet's text for its chronological imprecision and its fabrication in the interests of rhetorical ornamentation ('pour faire valoir un bon mot').[20] As the Ronsard scholar and critical editor of the *Vie de Ronsard*, Laumonier, observed of Binet: 'c'est un panégyriste posthume, qui substitue trop souvent le roman et la rhétorique à l'histoire.'[21]

Binet and the 'Elégie à Remy de Belleau' (1578): Rewriting Ronsard

In this second section, I shall analyse in some detail the rhetorical dimension of the *Vie de Ronsard*. My discussion will focus on three instances where Binet incorporates Ronsard's own poetry into his text, without giving any indication of provenance. To flesh out his portrait of Ronsard, Binet thus continued to follow the example of Ronsard's Mercury, the master of those marketplace tricksters who 'Jouants de gobelets font tours de passe-passes' (v. 148). As Ronsard's biographer, Binet was an imposter who transposed into the third person the first-person statements of his hero. By pillaging Ronsard's verse in this way, Binet sought to polish his own prose and secure for himself a reputation for eloquence and excellence in prose style.[22]

In what follows, I shall consider in some detail three episodes from Binet's narrative of his hero's infancy and early youth. Each of these examples rewrites Ronsard's autobiographical 'Elégie à Remy Belleau'; and each helps to fashion an image of Ronsard as a divinely anointed poet, who can trace his literary genealogy back through ancient precursors.[23] Clustered in the early part of the *Vie*, these incidents strengthen the perception of Ronsard as a poet-*vates*. Furthermore, other contemporary testimonies of Ronsard's life, such as Jacques Davy Du Perron's funerary oration, did not include this sequence of fortunate accidents.[24] The conspicuous position they occupy at the beginning of the biography thus constitutes Binet's contribution to the divinization of Ronsard.

Each of the three scenes involves a serious physical threat to Ronsard's person. Ronsard survived each event unscathed, and with his destiny as a great poet confirmed. Binet acknowledges that Ronsard did show promise as a courtier — the career his father intended him to follow. Still, in these passages, Binet intimates that the stamp of Ronsard's true vocation had been imprinted upon him since birth. No accident of fortune could see his hero deviate from this fixed course. Here, Binet defers to Ronsard's conception of the soul, rather than external circumstances, as determining an individual's profession:

Elle [l'âme] fait que les uns deviennent inventeurs
Des secrets plus cachez, les autres Orateurs,
Les autres Medecins: aux uns la Poësie
Imprime *brusquement* dedans la fantaisie[...][25]

In the *Discours des miseres de ce temps*, Ronsard articulated the similar notion that his professional identity did not reflect a response to chance events, but was rather the inevitable product of the exercise of his rational judgement and will in the light of his natural abilities.[26] By insisting on the ineluctability of Ronsard's career as a poet, Binet suggests that he could not have been a child of Mercury. Whilst Mercury prompts men to invent 'mille mestiers nouveaux,' Ronsard's nature consigned him to a single calling.

The mercurial Binet, however, systematically rewrites Ronsard's verse in his prose in ways which make it more rhetorical. In particular, his use of rhetorical amplification allows him to advertise his considerable abilities as a stylist. My first example relates an accident which took place on the day of Ronsard's baptism. Ronsard succinctly alludes to an early brush with death in the autobiographical elegy to Belleau: '[...] et presque je me vy | Tout aussi tost que né, de la Parque ravy' (vv. 45–46). Binet, however, embroiders on these two scant lines to create a vivid description of the scene of this drama.[27] His account contains a number of rhetorical flourishes which serve at once to reveal the poet's glorious destiny and to display the biographer's stylistic mastery:

> Mais peu s'en falut que le jour de sa naissance ne fut aussi le jour de son enterrement: car comme on le portoit baptizer du Chasteau de la Possonniere en l'Eglise du village de Cousture, celle qui le portoit, traversant un pré, le laissa tomber par mesgarde sur l'herbe et fleurs, qui le receurent plus doucement: et eut encor cet accident une autre rencontre qu'une Damoiselle qui portoit un vaisseau plein d'eau de roses, pensant ayder à receuillir l'enfant, luy renversa sur le chef une partie de l'eauë de senteur: qui fut un presage des bonnes odeurs dont il remplit toute la France, des fleurs de ses escris. (*Vie de Ronsard*, p. 4)

In Binet's much amplified version of the episode, the woman who carried Ronsard drops him inadvertently: 'par mesgarde'. Whereas the world of men has not yet learned to look out for Ronsard, Nature receives him 'plus doucement', cushioning his fall by the dense growth of grass and flowers in the meadow. Nature's protection first alerts the reader that a supernatural force may be operating here to ensure Ronsard's safety. Further such signs are to come. As if the single accident of dropping the infant were not enough, the mishap is compounded when a second servant tries to help pick him up: 'et eut encor cet accident une autre rencontre'. Still, against this backdrop of chance events, Binet's rhetoric transports the reader from the sublunary world, ruled by fortune, to a celestial province governed by destiny. Binet's florid comparison between the rose-water poured on to Ronsard's head and the future 'fleurs de ses escris' is especially interesting. Not only did it constitute a presage of greatness, it also alludes to a characteristic aspect of Ronsard's poetic genius: his 'copia' or abundance of expression. Although the servant spilled only a portion of the scented liquid ('une partie de l'eauë de senteur'), Ronsard manages to fill France with the perfume of his verse. Thus, in this first episode, Binet's prose glides seamlessly from the narration of what is meant to pass as biographical truth on to the figurative level of panegyric.

A further narrow escape from an untimely death occurred when the fifteen-year-old Ronsard's master Charles d'Orléans sent him on a diplomatic mission to Scotland.[28] After a storm-tossed crossing, Ronsard's ship was wrecked in port. Binet's description of this second near calamity similarly evokes an apotropaic power:

> Auquel voyage, pensant tirer en Ecosse, le vaisseau auquel il estoit fut tellement, durant trois jours, pourmené par la tempeste, qu'il cuida sur la coste d'Angleterre estre brisé contre un rocher, mal-heur qui fut seulement differé, pour sauver principalement nostre futur Arion d'un tel naufrage: car le navire qui avoit eschappé tant de dangers, apres avoir laissé sa charge sur la rade d'Ecosse, sans peril fit naufrage au port, brisé et enfondré avec tout le bagage, que le plus grand soin de sauver la vie laissa à la mercy des flots. (*Vie de Ronsard*, p. 6)

Again, Binet has borrowed from Ronsard's 'Elégie à Remy Belleau', this time staying very close to his source:

> Et depuis en Escosse, où la tempeste grande
> [...] cuida faire toucher,
> poussée aux bords Anglois, la nef contre un rocher.
> Plus de trois jours entiers dura ceste tempeste,
> D'eau, de gresle et d'esclairs nous menassant la teste,
> A la fin arrivez sans nul danger au port,
> La nef en cent morceaux se rompt contre le bord,
> Nous laissant sur la rade, et point n'y eut de perte,
> Sinon elle qui fut des flots salez couverte,
> Et le bagage espars que le vent secouoit,
> Et qui servoit flottant aux ondes de jouet. (vv. 64–74)

The only significant change Binet has made to the 'Elégie à Belleau' is his explicit reference to forces at work to protect Ronsard. His safe arrival in port comes about not by chance, but by design: 'pour sauver principalement nostre futur Arion d'un tel naufrage'. The comparison to the mythical poet Arion both glorifies Ronsard and elevates Binet's prose. Removing Ronsard's prosaic description of the stormy weather with its rain, hail and lightening gives a further dimension of sublimity to Binet's text.

The third instance of rewriting of the 'Elégie à Belleau' is Binet's version of the onset of Ronsard's deafness, which was evident on his return from diplomatic service in Germany. According to both the 'Elégie à Belleau' and the *Vie*, this disability sealed Ronsard's poetic destiny. He could no longer hope to be successful as a courtier, who would need his hearing to distinguish himself in elegant conversation. Again, Binet amplifies Ronsard's much briefer account. Ronsard attributes his deafness only vaguely to '[...] ne sçay quel destin' (v. 80). Binet, however, provides a more detailed explanation.[29] In Binet's account, Ronsard falls ill because of the foul wine he drank while in Germany, and because of the incommodities of travel: bad roads and sea-sickness. Binet goes on to provide a medical explanation for Ronsard's condition: 'plusieurs humeurs grossieres luy monterent au cerveau, tellement qu'elles luy causerent une defluxion, et puis une fievre tierce dont il devient sourdault [...]'.[30] The profusion of medical detail endows Binet's prose with greater persuasive effect. Like the shipwreck episode, the tale of Ronsard's illness give rise to a comparison with an ancient poet:

> Ainsi en advint à ce divin Homere, qui sur la fin de ses voyages, s'estant embarqué avec le marinier Mentes, pour apprendre les diverses façons de peuples, et la nature des choses ayant abordé l'Isle d'Ithaque eut un catherre sur les yeux qui luy fit perdre la veüe estant arrivé à Colophone.[31]

Although the comparison does not occur in the 'Elégie', Binet's source does lie in Ronsard's verse. In the *Reponse aux injures et calomnies* (vv. 235–42), Ronsard had compared his own and Du Bellay's deafness with Homer's blindness as a sign of the Muses' favour.[32] Binet, however, has elaborated on the parallel in yet another demonstration of rhetorical amplification: varying expressions at the same time as he develops ideas. First, Binet compares the two poets on more than one level: not only were their maladies similar (blindness and deafness), but so too are the accidental circumstances under which they came about (while travelling). Second, Binet insists on the difference between Ronsard and Homer:

> Voila comment deux grans Poëtes, par un presque semblable sort se virent privez de sens fort necessaires: Homere les escrits duquel tout le monde devoit voir, et lire si soigneusement, de celuy de la veüe: et Ronsard, dont la douce cadence des vers devoit estre recueillie des plus delicates oreilles du monde de celuy de l'ouye.[33]

Although their fate was 'presque semblable', their verse held a distinct form of appeal. Whereas Homer had the whole world for his audience, the nature of Ronsard's verse restricts his readership to a select few: the 'plus delicates oreilles du monde'. Thus Binet ensures that Ronsard's Greek precursor did not overshadow him.

Poet-*vates* into Courtier–Poet: Binet's 1597 Additions to the *Vie de Ronsard*

Having considered Binet's rewriting of Ronsard's poetry as a demonstration of the biographer's capacity for rhetorical amplification, I should like, in the last section of this chapter, to look at two 1597 additions to the *Vie de Ronsard*. Each represents Ronsard as socially and professionally ambitious. As we have seen, in the passages Binet took from the 'Elégie à Belleau', he portrays Ronsard as divinely protected — and, by extension, divinely inspired. Such a view accords well with Ronsard's own neo-Platonic conception of the poet.[34] In these later additions to Binet's text, though, we see Ronsard in an altogether different light. Here, he is adept in the art of courtiership, skilled at attracting the attention of the sovereign, and even ready to take his inspiration not from poetic *furor*, but from royal suggestion. This Ronsard begins to resemble the 'subtil et cauteleux' figure of Mercury, who can dupe an audience with his showmanship and who traffics in verse.

The first anecdote reveals Ronsard's concern with maintaining his place of favour at court despite competition from other artists. It features in a discussion of Ronsard's satiric verse, composed, Binet asserts, with the express permission of Charles IX, the king under whom Ronsard enjoyed the greatest favour. One of Ronsard's satires, 'La Truelle crossée', reproached the king for giving benefices to masons and other 'viles personnes' whose lack of education made them unworthy of such elevation.[35] Ronsard directed his satire particularly at the architect currently enjoying royal favour, Philibert de l'Orme, responsible for the Tuileries palace. By the mid-1560s, de l'Orme, like Ronsard himself, had cumulated an impressive number of benefices including three abbeys, as well as several royal offices.[36] The enactment of the conflict between Ronsard and de l'Orme exemplifies the theatrical techniques of intrigue known as 'practiques' which came to characterize political culture at the French court during the latter half of the sixteenth century.[37] Complex rhetorical devices which combined gesture, scenic backdrop — including public spaces — and words, such 'practiques' communicated politically charged messages.

Binet relates how, one day, de l'Orme sought to avenge himself on Ronsard for the satire against him. De l'Orme closed the gate of the Tuileries to the poet, preventing him from joining the queen mother who was enjoying a promenade in the garden with a group of courtiers. Ronsard, remaining very much on his guard, straightaway contrived an impressive riposte. As Binet commented, the poet could be 'assez piquant et mordant quand il vouloit'. With some chalk, Ronsard wrote on the gates an inscription in Latin capitals. This contained an abbreviated quotation from an epigram by Ausonius: 'Fort. Reverent. Habe.' Ronsard then infiltrated the Tuileries to catch up with the royal party. When the assembled courtiers exited from the gardens a short while later, the queen mother, Catherine de Médicis, having noticed Ronsard's graffito, stopped to ask its meaning. Ronsard explained, but only after de l'Orme had blurted out his guess that it pertained to him. As Binet pointed out, being ignorant of Latin, de l'Orme had misconstrued the inscription because he had read it in French and interpreted it to mean: 'fort révérend abbé'. Ronsard's revenge against de l'Orme was thus an extremely cunningly crafted 'practique'. De l'Orme revealed his own ignorance, both of the Latin language, and of the learned quotation. From book nineteen of Ausonius's epigrams, the line cited by Ronsard exhorted those who had experienced a rapid social elevation to show due gratitude to Fortune.[38] The queen mother helped Ronsard to complete the 'practique' by reminding de l'Orme, after all had shared a good laugh at his expense, that the Tuileries were dedicated to the Muses, and should thus never be closed to poets. The entire anecdote shows Ronsard to be a master practitioner of the art of courtly performance. He has judged his audience perfectly and anticipated their reactions. The presence of the queen mother ensured that his message would not be lost. De l'Orme's humiliation would have been the more complete since his own building provided the backdrop for it. Taking a humble piece of chalk, the poet easily overwrote the builder and came up trumps as a courtier.

The second anecdote I should like to discuss, also a 1597 addition, involves similar issues of patronage and the status of the artist. Here, Binet revealed how a royal request motivated Ronsard's adoption of a particular style in his late love poetry. In the original version of the *Vie de Ronsard*, Binet had made no mention of any of Ronsard's love poetry posterior to the *Continuation des Amours* of 1555. Only in 1597 did Binet provide a full account of the genesis of Ronsard's final collection of love poems, the 1584 *Sonnets pour Hélène*. Written in Ronsard's old age, they represented the apogee of his career as love poet. Indeed, as Binet noted, Ronsard intended them as the crowning glory of his entire œuvre: 'il voulut finir et couronner ses œuvres par les *Sonnets d'Helene*'.[39] Binet's presentation of these poems may have been conditioned by the concern of their addressee, Hélène de Surgères, for her honour.[40] Thus, in the 1587 *Vie*, when Binet first briefly mentioned the sonnets, he insisted on their purely Platonic inspiration: 'et luy a ceste gentille Damoiselle servy de blanc, pour viser et non pour tirer ou attaindre, l'ayant aimée chastement'.[41] While the 1597 text continued to insist on the chastity of Ronsard's love for Hélène, it also suggested that Hélène did not herself furnish the sole inspiration for the poems. Rather, Catherine de Médicis, whose lady-in-waiting Hélène was, had commissioned the collection.[42] According to Binet's account, a public reading of one of Ronsard's 'chaste et modeste' poems to Hélène had whetted the queen mother's appetite for more such verse. Binet thus represented Ronsard as a poet whose work obtained a favourable hearing at court and even in the presence of royalty. Not only did this public reading prompt the commission of the collection, but, Binet tells us, it also determined its style. Catherine specifically requested that Ronsard should imitate Petrarch 'comme plus conforme à son âge, et à la gravité de son sçavoir'. This anecdote, then, emphasized Ronsard's status and prestige as a court poet.[43]

That Binet highlighted Catherine's role in the production of the *Sonnets pour Hélène* and Ronsard's eager submission to her request is initially puzzling. Such a presentation of the relationship between poet and royal patron appears paradoxical since Binet had just cited the poet's complaint about having to write poetry on command: 'Il me dit maintesfois, que plusieurs pieces de ses Amours et des Mascarades avoient esté forgées sur le commandement des grans, voulant dire qu'il avoit souvent forcé sa Minerve et n'y avoit pris grand plaisir'.[44] Binet thus gives the reader the impression of blatant self-contradiction in Ronsard's attitude. Rather than being an inadvertent consequence of his revision of the *Vie*, I would argue that Binet's depiction of Ronsard's shifting stance has the effect of further transforming the poet-*vates* into proteiform courtier–poet. Binet shows the reader a Ronsard who might on occasion grumble about having to curry favour with those in power, but who ultimately remained too agile a courtier to let any opportunity for self-aggrandizement pass him by. The final version of Binet's biography, then, portrays a Ronsard with great capacity for accommodation and flexibility.

To conclude, then, the architecture of the *Vie de Ronsard* testifies to Binet's divinization of his hero as 'Prince et pere de nos poëtes'. Binet continued to endow Ronsard with quasi-divine status as a poet when he rewrote a number of passages from the autobiographical 'Elégie à Belleau'. Here, though, he did not concern himself simply with exalting Ronsard, but with showcasing his own skill at rhetorical amplification. Binet's theft of Ronsard's poetry to constitute the material of his biography is just one way in which he behaved like Ronsardian Mercury. Binet also assimilated Ronsard himself to this inventive, quick-witted god when he revised his *Vie* to highlight Ronsard's adroitness at the art of courtly performance. But this depiction of Ronsard as poet–courtier also has the endorsement of Ronsard's own verse. For instance, in the 'Responce aux injures', Ronsard furnishes an account of his daily activities from sunrise to sunset.[45] This narrative ostensibly performs the function of an apologia attesting Ronsard's personal piety and his studious existence as a poet:

> M'esveillant au matin, devant que faire rien
> J'invoque l'Eternel le pere de tout bien,
> Le priant humblement de me donner sa grace,
> [...]
> Apres je sors du lict, et quand je suis vestu
> Je me range à l'estude et apprens la vertu,
> Composant et lisant suivant ma destinée,
> Qui s'est dés mon enfance aux Muses enclinée
> ('Responce aux injures', vv. 476–78; 485–88)

However, as Langer has shown, a rather different self emerges from Ronsard's description of what he does on inclement days:

> Je cherche compagnie, ou je joue à la Prime,
> Je voltige ou je saute, ou je lutte ou j'escrime,
> Je dy le mot pour rire, et à la verité
> Je ne loge chez moy trop de severité.
> ('Responce aux injures', vv. 511–14)

This Ronsard bears comparison to the young Gargantua, the very type of the courtly young nobleman who not only takes part in the kind of physical activity appropriate to a knight, but who carefully maintains an affable demeanour for the amusement of his prince.[46] And indeed, in the 'Responce' as a whole, Ronsard reveals himself to be a courtier able to accommodate himself to circumstances by adapting his *ethos* to serve the rhetorical needs of the moment, even going so far as to declare that he would be capable of surviving the destruction of the Catholic church.[47] Ronsard's own fascination with the profit to be won by shape-changing and mutability finds further echo in the 'Hymne de Mercure', where the poet had identified Mercury not only with eloquence but also with the transformational art of alchemy. As an apprentice poet, we saw how Binet built his career on his association with the 'prince des poètes', Ronsard. Having largely abandoned the cultivation of the Muses to pursue promotion in the field of law, Binet still depended on Ronsard to secure his own glory by providing the subject for the rhetorical art of biography.

Notes to Chapter 3

1. Benedikte Andersson discusses the mimetic aspect of the *Vie de Ronsard*: in his biography, Binet uses Ronsard's life and work to construct a literary persona for himself as poet. She does not focus, however, on the adjustments Binet makes to the Ronsardian material in the interests of his own self-fashioning as flexible courtier-poet. 'Du code autobiographique à la lecture biographique: Claude Binet, lecteur de Ronsard', in *Problématiques de l'autobiographie*, Littérales, 33 (Paris: Centre des Sciences de la Littérature Française, 2004), pp. 33–48.
2. Marc-Antoine de Muret, *Commentaires au premier livre des «Amours» de Ronsard*, ed. by J. Chomarat, M.-M. Fragonard and G. Mathieu Castellani (Geneva: Droz, 1985); Remy Belleau,

Commentaire au second livre des «Amours» de Ronsard, ed. by M.-M. Fontaine and F. Lecercle (Geneva: Droz, 1986). Andersson compares Binet's biography to the commentary genre (pp. 43–45).

3. Paul Laumonier has documented how Ronsard's works formed the major source for Binet's biography. Laumonier, 'Introduction,' in *La Vie de P. de Ronsard de Claude Binet (1586)*. Edition critique avec introduction et commentaire historique et critique (Paris: Hachette, 1910). See also Andersson, pp. 34–38.
4. Claude Binet, *La Vie de P. de Ronsard de Claude Binet (1586)*, ed. by Paul Laumonier, p. 45.
5. *Vie de Ronsard*, p. 50.
6. On the 'Hymne de Mercure', see Daniel Ménager, *Ronsard. Le Roi, le Poète et les Hommes* (Geneva: Droz, 1979), pp. 16–128.
7. Ronsard, 'Hymne x De Mercure, à Claude Binet, Beauvaisin', in *Œuvres complètes*, ed. by Jean Céard, Daniel Ménager, and Michel Simonin, 2 vols (Paris: Gallimard, 1993), II, 612–17 (vv. 199–202).
8. Laumonier, 'Introduction', in *Vie de Ronsard*, p. xviii.
9. *Vie de Ronsard*, p. 50.
10. Ullrich Langer, *Vertu du discours, discours de la vertu. Littérature et philosophie morale au XVIe siècle en France* (Geneva: Droz, 1999), p. 29 and pp. 75–92.
11. Cicero, *De inventione*, trans. by H. M. Hubbell (London: Heinemann; Cambridge, MA: Harvard University Press, 1949), 2.53.159–2.54.165.
12. Laumonier, 'Introduction', p. xiii.
13. Binet, 'Diverses poësies', in Jean Bastier de La Péruse, *Les Œuvres de J. Bastier de La Péruse* (Paris: Nicolas Bonfons, 1573), fols. 140–78.
14. After La Péruse's death, Remy Belleau replaced him in the list of Pléiade poets.
15. Binet, *Les Plaisirs de la vie rustique et solitaire* (Paris: veuve Lucas Breyer, 1583).
16. Pibrac, *Les Plaisirs de la vie rustique* (Paris: Federic Morel, 1574 [1575]).
17. In Vauquelin's *Art poëtique*. Jean Vauquelin de la Fresnaye, *L'Art poëtique de Vauquelin de la Fresnaye*, ed. by Georges Pellissier (Paris: Garnier, 1885), book 3, vv. 253–54, p. 140.
18. *Les plaisirs de la vie rustique qui sont divers poemes sur ce sujet extraits de plusieurs excellens Autheurs de nostre temps* (Paris, 1583).
19. Ronsard, 'Discours à Loys des Masures', in *Œuvres complètes*, II, 1017–20. Laumonier, 'Introduction', p. xxiv.
20. Laumonier, 'Introduction', p. viii and p. 70.
21. Laumonier, 'Introduction', p. x.
22. This is ironic, since, as Binet himself noted, Ronsard castigated those meagre versifiers who believed that they had created a masterpiece if they transposed prose into verse. See Ronsard, 'Abrégé de l'Art poëtique', in *Œuvres complètes*, II, 1184.
23. Ronsard, 'Elégie XVI', in *Œuvres complètes*, II, 371–72.
24. Jacques Davy Du Perron, *Oraison funebre sur la mort de Monsieur de Ronsard* (Paris: Federic Morel, 1586).
25. Ronsard, 'L'Excellence de l'esprit de l'Homme', in *Œuvres complètes*, II, 839, (vv. 63–66, emphasis mine).
26. Langer, *Vertu du discours*, p. 77. See Cicero, *De officiis*, trans. by Walter Miller (London: Heinemann; New York: MacMillan, 1913), 1.30.107–1.33.121.
27. On the possible historical veracity of this episode, see Laumonier, 'Introduction', p. 68.
28. See Michel Dassonville, *Ronsard. Etude historique et littéraire*, 5 vols (Geneva: Droz, 1968–90), I, 100–06.
29. Du Perron did not give a precise reason (natural or supernatural) for the illness. George Critton blamed the storm off the coast of Scotland, thus linking the two fateful accidents (quoted by Laumonier, 'Introduction', p. 81). Critton, *Laudatio funebris habita in exequiis Petri Ronsardi* (Paris: A. D'Auvel, 1586). Jacques Velliard's account, which blamed the rigours of Ronsard's nomadic existence during his travels, is probably the closest to Binet's. Jacques Velliard, *Petri Ronsard, poetæ gallici laudatio funebris* (Paris: Denis Du Pré, 1586).
30. *Vie de Ronsard*, p. 7.
31. *Vie de Ronsard*, p. 7.

32. Laumonier, 'Introduction', p. 82.
33. *Vie de Ronsard*, p. 8. Binet's insistence on the auditory reception of Ronsard, as opposed to the visual reception of Homer, recalls the popularity of musical settings for the former's verse. See Jules Tiersot, *Ronsard et la musique de son temps* (Leipzig: Breitkopf und Haertel, 1903) and Louis Perceau and Geneviève Thibault, *Bibliographie des poésies de P. de Ronsard mises en musique au XVIe siècle* (Paris: Droz, 1941).
34. See, for example, 'Ode à Michel de l'Hospital' (*Les Odes*, I.10), in *Œuvres complètes*, I, 626–50.
35. Laumonier discusses and rejects various possible identifications for the poems Binet mentions ('Introduction', pp. 170–71).
36. De L'Orme held the offices of 'Conseiller et aumônier général du roi' and 'Surintendant des bâtiments royaux'. See Laumonier, 'Introduction', p. 171. Anthony Blunt, *Philibert de l'Orme* (London: A. Zwemmer, 1958).
37. Xavier Le Person, *'Practiques' et 'Practiqueurs': La Vie politique à la fin du règne de Henri III (1584–1589)* (Geneva: Droz, 2002).
38. 'Fortunam reverenter habe, quicunque repente/Dives ab exili progrediere loco'. Ausonius, *Epigrammata*, 2, vv. 7–8 ('Exhortatio ad modestiam'), in Ausonius, *Decimi magni Ausonii Burdigalensis opuscula*, ed. by Sesto Prete (Leipzig: Teubner, 1978), p. 287.
39. *Vie de Ronsard*, p. 26.
40. Laumonier, p. xxxvi.
41. *Vie de Ronsard*, p. 25.
42. With the cunning of an accomplished courtier, Binet waited until after Catherine's death (1589) to add this information, thus avoiding the possibility that she might contest the veracity of this assertion. Laumonier, p. xxxvi.
43. The precise wording of Binet's presentation of the royal request and Ronsard's reception of it makes yet more explicit the power relationships underlying the production of the sonnets. After Catherine exhorted Ronsard to write this work, the poet took his queen's 'conseil' as 'permission, ou plustost commandement' (*Vie de Ronsard*, p. 26).
44. *Vie de Ronsard*, p. 25.
45. Ronsard, 'Responce aux injures', in *Œuvres complètes*, II, 1055–56, (vv. 477–524).
46. Langer, *Vertu du discours*, p. 92.
47. Ronsard, 'Responce aux injures', in *Œuvres complètes*, II, 1064–65, (vv. 891–99). Langer, *Vertu du discours*, pp. 85–87.

Figure 4. Portrait of Ramus from Ramus, *Testamentum P. Rami* (Paris: J. Richer, 1576).

CHAPTER 4

Medicine and Method in Nicolas de Nancel's *Petri Rami Vita* (1599)

Once a year, at about the time of the summer solstice, the internationally renowned philosopher, rhetorician and pedagogue Pierre de la Ramée, or Ramus (1515–72) took a bath. His hands, face and beard, though, were the object of more frequent ablutions, as he washed these body parts in white wine diluted with water twice a day before meals, or at least once in the morning. So we learn from his one-time pupil, then colleague and secretary, Nicolas de Nancel (1539–1610), who recorded these facts about Ramus in 1599. To illuminate why he did so will be the aim of the current chapter.

Nancel was not writing a treatise on personal hygiene, but a biographical memorial to his late teacher, whom he clearly regarded as a scholarly colossus.[1] How Ramus bathed and washed, then, might seem a trivial, mundane, even demeaning piece of information to include in a biography. But such particulars were central to another type of discourse in the sixteenth century: that of the medical profession, of which Nancel was a member. Detailed advice on the modalities of washing was generally proffered by contemporary authors of health manuals, who followed the Galenic model in considering baths a crucial part of health.[2] In what follows, I shall contend that the biographical representation of Ramus in the *Vita Rami* reflects a particular facet of Nancel's own existence: his knowledge of *materia medica* and his long experience of clinical practice. I shall argue that his familiarity with Galenic notions of regimen as well as medical theories of physiognomy significantly informed his portrayal of Ramus.

Whereas Nancel's medical identity remains a covert, shaping force behind the *Vita Rami*, his role as Ramus's anointed intellectual heir is everywhere foregrounded in it. This text, like Binet's *Vie de Ronsard* discussed in the previous chapter, accords a prominent role to the life and achievements of the biographer himself. Indeed, it would not be unreasonable to assert that the authors of both works reveal a preoccupation as much with their own glory as with that of the subject they strove to immortalize. In the case of each biographer, a generation separated him from his subject, whom he first encountered as mentor or teacher. Unlike Binet, who exaggerated the intimacy and duration of his relationship with Ronsard, Nancel could truthfully assert that his knowledge of Ramus was based on a close familiarity of more than two decades, first as his student and then as his colleague. Still, Nancel took advantage of the history of their association to intercalate an account of his own life into his biography of Ramus. Although separated by religion — Ramus was a Protestant whereas his biographer remained a devout Catholic — Nancel willingly bridged the confessional divide by defending Ramus against charges of iconoclasm and providing a sympathetic account of his subject's martyrdom in the St. Bartholomew's Day massacre.[3] By effacing any hint of confessional tension between them, Nancel facilitated the identification between biographer and subject.

Thus, when introducing a discussion of the Collège de Presles of which Ramus was principal and where he lived much of his life, Nancel wrote that he treated this topic because Presles was the institution which nourished his own studies.[4] There follows a summary version of Nancel's own educational curriculum, from his time as a young bursary student up until he took the degree of doctor of philosophy and beyond, when he became a teacher of Greek and Latin himself. In a self-aggrandizing comparison, Nancel noted that the length of time he spent with Ramus equalled that Aristotle was said to have spent with Plato. In the *Vita Rami*, Nancel also draws attention to his indispensable service to Ramus in the classroom. Here, he would stand behind Ramus while he was lecturing and tug on his coat to alert him if he made a mistake.[5] More crucially, Nancel dwells at length on his scholarly collaboration with Ramus. In trumpeting his own important contribution to the Ramist publishing enterprise, he is in no way reticent. On the contrary, Nancel tells how he assisted Ramus with his commentary on Vergil, as well as playing an instrumental role in the elaboration of Ramus's Greek grammar. Ramus assigned the task of editing his lectures on Cicero to Nancel, who was to publish them under his own name — although Nancel relates that this manuscript was unfortunately stolen.[6] Furthermore, Nancel even uses the *Vita Rami* to support an explicit identification between himself and Ramus. Nancel quotes Ramus as jokingly calling him 'another little Ramus', who would naturally assume his teacher's mantle, unless he married and opted for another path in life, outside the university establishment.[7]

As it happened, the Nancel would soon choose to exile himself from Presles, the intellectual coterie of Ramus and the academic scene altogether. In the 1560s, with the outbreak of the French Wars of Religion, Nancel left Paris and his beloved teacher Ramus, for Douai, then a stronghold of the Counter-Reformation.[8] At the new University of Douai, founded in 1562 by the Spanish king Philip II to fight heresy, Nancel took up the study of medicine.[9] Although he had taught at the university of Paris and, later, at that of Douai (1562–64), Nancel never occupied a university chair. Instead, he remained outside of the academic establishment, and made his living as a professional practising physician. By 1568, he was in full time medical practice in the northern town of Soissons.[10] After a failed attempt to obtain a post as a royal physician to Charles IX, in 1570 Nancel settled in Tours, where he would prosper for the next seventeen years treating the local population before ultimately becoming personal physician to the abbess of Fontrevault, Eléonore de Bourbon.[11]

It was thus in around 1582, whilst he was professionally occupied as a practising physician in Tours that Nancel probably composed his *Vita Rami*, ten years after Ramus's death.[12] At the same time, Nancel was intellectually immersed in the world of learned medicine, transcribing, emending and annotating a great number of medical texts, including treatises by ancient Greek and Arabic authors such as Hippocrates (*c*.450–370 BCE), Galen (129–216) and Avicenna (or Ibn Sina, 980–1037).[13] Although Nancel addressed the *Vita Rami* to fellow students of Ramus, and although, as we have seen, he explicitly presents himself in it as Ramus's intellectual heir, he actually composed the biography some time after he had left the rarefied environment of the Collège de Presles. The intervening decades spent in medical scholarship and clinical practice left their indelible mark on the *Vita Rami*. As a biographer, Nancel remained a learned physician. This helps to explain why his biography of his teacher Ramus is replete with lively, closely observed detail which appeals strongly to the reader's eyes and ears. The clinical precision of Nancel's observation of Ramus's physical person and hygiene regimen is significantly indebted to the world of contemporary Galenic medical learning and practice. Medical discourse informs the biography and shapes Nancel's representation of Ramus. However, this discourse remains a subtext in the biography, for Nancel does not explicitly identify himself as a professional physician in the *Vita Rami*.

Medical Discourses in the *Vita Rami*

Whereas Nancel did not explicitly write as a learned physician in the *Vita Rami*, in the preface to his magnum opus, the vast *Analogia microcosmi ad macrocosmion* (1611) he was keen to establish his professional credentials as a medical man. Intriguingly, what Nancel argued in this text about the way physicians write is reminiscent of his description of his biographical methodology in the *Vita Rami*. In the *Analogia*, over and above his considerable theoretical knowledge of anatomy and physiology, Nancel vaunts the value of his personal experience and observations gathered over some forty years of medical practice.[14] In particular, he notes how physicians write clearly and persuasively because they have access to the experiential evidence provided by the eyes — *experientia*. Nancel's stance is in keeping with the increasingly descriptive approach scholars have noted in Renaissance medicine, which, compared to its ancient and medieval precursors, devoted considerably greater attention to the individual and the particular.[15] The ideal doctor, as described by one contemporary physician, was 'a man of judgement who gained understanding from careful observation of patients which then led to a reasoned choice of remedies'.[16] When it came to establishing his authority as biographer in the preface to the *Vita Rami*, I would argue that Nancel tacitly suggests his own conformity with this ideal, although without alluding to his membership of the medical profession. Here, addressing himself to fellow students of Ramus, Nancel claims to offer his biography as a kind of 'aide-mémoire' to those who had the privilege of knowing Ramus. For those who had no personal acquaintance with Ramus, Nancel's work would, he declared, put the philosopher before their eyes. As the precise wording of the preface indicates, Nancel founded his biographical authority on the strength of visual, indeed clinical, observation of his subject:

> [...] for those who neither heard nor saw him, pointing him out, introducing him, and making him known, since I myself saw him, heard him and knew him well. I set out point by point, as far as I can remember them, all the facts which I observed during the period of nearly twenty years when I lodged with him [...].[17]

Nancel's exaltation of experience and observation here is equally concordant with his formation in Ramist principles of textual interpretation and commentary. As Ramus wrote in his *Lectures on the liberal arts*:

> Experience gives rise to an art; inexperience breeds only temerity, and no rule should be included in an art which is not observed and induced from the use and observation of true examples.[18]

We may thus choose to attribute the championing of *experientia* in the preface to the *Vita* either to Nancel's medical training or to his adherence to Ramism.

However, no such ambiguity attaches to Nancel's exhaustive depiction of Ramus's daily habits, the 'régime de vie' which we encounter at roughly the mid-point of the biography (pp. 226–46). This lengthy section certainly betrays the influence on Nancel of contemporary medical discourse, and in particular of Galenic dietetics. Moreover, as we shall see, Nancel's medical background also provided him with a template for representing Ramus's moral character. The specificity of Nancel's description of Ramus's eating habits, his daily exercise regimen, annual bathing ritual and even his dress and how he chose to furnish his home is without precedent in any of the other contemporary accounts of Ramus, or indeed in any of the other biographies under discussion here.[19] In its minutiae it reminds one of the much-analysed sequence in Montaigne's 'De l'experience' in which he tells us about his table habits.[20] Not only does Montaigne disclose which foods he prefers (melons, sauces, fish) and those he is not terribly fond of (salads), he goes on to provide an account of his wardrobe according to the seasons, his sleep habits and even the workings of his bowels. Jean Céard has analysed the medical subtext present in this seemingly anecdotal, confessional episode, arguing that 'Montaigne ne peut se raconter qu'en s'appropriant le langage des médecins'.[21] Even the very principles upon which Montaigne founded his questioning of medical wisdom and his rejection of the authority of physicians accord with contemporary 'régimes de santé'. Montaigne's view that, in the preservation of health, individuals should adopt personal habit and 'volupté' and not abstract general rules as their guide has, as Céard observes, a basis in the Hippocratic-Galenic teachings current amongst sixteenth-century learned physicians like Ambroise Paré.[22]

As for Nancel, his account of Ramus's daily routine is likewise constituted in dialogue with contemporary medical discourse, and in particular with the teachings of Galenic medicine in regard to regimen. I have noted how Nancel founded his claim to reliability as a witness to Ramus's life on strictly empirical grounds, because of his *experientia* of his subject. But, I would contend, he did not reproduce this knowledge later as a pure empiricist, without recourse to a pre-existing mental grid. Nancel claims that he 'saw, heard and knew' Ramus well because of the twenty years he spent observing him at close quarters. However, he wrote his *Vita Rami* some ten years after the philosopher's death, and after he had devoted twenty years to the theory and practice of medicine. Therefore the sensory particulars Nancel had gathered whilst a student of Ramus would necessarily have been reorganized, in recollection, according to the patterns of observation familiar to the practising physician. In these patterns, Nancel would have been guided by the tradition, in existence since Hippocratic times and given further elaboration by Galen, whereby the maintenance of health in a patient was a matter of daily vigilance in certain matters: the notion of 'diet' or 'regimen'. For Hippocrates and later Galen, 'diet' referred not just to food and drink, but also to baths, physical exercise, dress and the environment (including climate and household furnishings).

The elements included in this conception of regimen were eventually systematized, by medieval physicians, as the six non-naturals, termed thus because they were external to the body. The six non-naturals included: air; food and drink; exercise (including sexual activity); rest, sleep and wakefulness; bodily evacuations; and the passions of the soul.[23] That the non-naturals were essential to the preservation of health remained the dominant view in university medicine during the sixteenth century and would have formed the backbone of Nancel's education in medical practice. Proper management of the six non-naturals in the light of individual temperament determined a person's wellbeing.[24] The key to good health was moderation in all things, according to the Aristotelian concept of the golden mean. For the sixteenth-century physician, excessive asceticism, but more usually, overindulgence, inevitably caused disease. Indeed, Galen cited Hippocrates's prescription for the healthy life as: 'Labour, food, drink, sleep, sex — moderation in all' (*Epidemics* 6.6.2).[25] As his primary task, the physician should therefore observe carefully his patient's behaviour with regard to each of these categories in order to recommend a suitable course of treatment. Galenists, for example, stressed the importance of beginning with only mild remedies which might include a minor change in diet or sleep habits. Training in careful observation of these areas of human activity and experience would thus have been a crucial element in the formation of a successful physician.[26] In his medical practice, then, Nancel would have been accustomed to taking note of and asking questions about precisely these sorts of matters.

We should not be surprised, therefore, to find that Nancel devotes considerable attention in the *Vita Rami* to the non-naturals, with the exception of air and bodily evacuations. Nancel's inclusion of such information betokened not simply a lively curiosity or the biographer's flair for the anecdotal, but more significantly the mental habits formed over many years of medical practice. The medical framework which structures Nancel's narration of Ramus's habits also relates bodily health to moral character. Because moderation was key to the Galenic conception of health, Nancel presents a Ramus who consistently strove to exercise prudent self-regulation and adhere to the middle way. As mentioned in the previous chapter, temperance was also one of the four *habitus laudabiles* — the permanent dispositions of character to be praised by the orator as cardinal virtues — inventoried by Cicero.[27]

In terms of the first of the non-naturals, food and drink, Nancel gave a detailed account of Ramus's eating habits, noting in particular the frugality and haste of his typical lunch, which might include boiled mutton or veal in a white sauce, some diluted wine, and cheese, and finally some seasonal fruit.[28] The order in which Ramus consumed these foods, and which Nancel carefully chronicles, is precisely that recommended by the authors of contemporary health manuals for optimum digestion.[29] After lunch, Ramus would rise from the table and take a short walk, only returning to his studies after an interval of a couple of hours, just as the learned doctors ordered.[30] Ramus's usual fare at dinner was more substantial, with several different sorts of meat, both boiled and roasted, and he lingered at table longer, conversing on philosophical topics with his guests.[31] In consuming a heartier dinner and a lighter lunch, Ramus followed the ancient advice, which crops up again in the sixteenth-century medical literature on regimen, that, since rest aided digestion, one should eat most at the evening meal, when one was closest to sleep.[32] None of the other biographies we have been studying here provides any detailed information about alimentary practices, which were an increasingly prominent part of both learned and popular medical literature in the second half of the sixteenth century.[33]

Ramus's regimen of physical exercise too was noted by Nancel. In addition to circumambulating the Collège de Presles twice daily on inspection tours, Ramus also regularly played handball two or three times a week after lunch with one other person.[34] So important was this game to Ramus that he even had a private court built at home. Nancel wrote that he did this in order to prevent people from watching him play: presumably Ramus feared his professorial dignity would suffer should anyone see him engaged in sport. But we need not necessarily assume that, by exposing this secret about Ramus, Nancel is trying to cut the great professor down to size. On the contrary, from the perspective of contemporary learned and popular medicine, in Ramus's dedication to this game, he was not only seeing to his bodily health, but also to that of his intellect. Galen had devoted an entire treatise to the praise of just such a game as ideal for the care of both body and soul. Authors of 'régimes de vie' in the later sixteenth century invariably referred to Galen's *The Exercise with the Small Ball* in their sections on exercise, where they singled out its benefits for the intellect as well as the body.[35] Moreover, the widespread diffusion and interest of Galen's treatise is attested by its translation into French in 1599, by coincidence the same year as the publication of the *Vita Rami*.[36]

As for sexual activity, Nancel was circumspect in his remarks about this side of Ramus's life, alluding to some malicious gossip about Ramus's violation of the celibacy required of him in his position as a college principal. However, although Nancel defends Ramus as naturally chaste, he is equally concerned to suggest that he was not unnaturally abstinent. To this end, Nancel asserts that Ramus had 'some human feelings, even in this matter' and claimed that he occasionally visited 'one little woman or another in the district' in order to satisfy his natural sexual urges.[37] Keen to show Ramus's pursuit of the golden mean in carnal matters in addition to everything else, Nancel reports a conversation in which Ramus confessed that he considered himself no longer suited to marriage, having passed the appropriate age for it. As Nancel further divulges, Ramus actively moderated his sexual urges by always sleeping on a rough blanket or hard straw and never on a feather mattress. The heat generated by a feather bed, Nancel sagely commented, affects one's limbs in such a way as to bring on pollution and erotic dreams.[38]

Sleep and wakefulness is another of the Galenic non-naturals which Nancel discusses at some length, in terms which again recall the medical literature on regimen. Nancel reveals that Ramus was accustomed to take a siesta after lunch in summer,[39] but that sleep did not always come easily to him at night owing to overwork and anxiety about his enemies.[40] To overcome his insomnia and ensure a regular sleep pattern, Ramus would send for a boy to read to him for an hour or two. When a young scholar at the Collège de Navarre in Paris, Ramus had such zeal for his studies that he devoted scarcely three hours a night to sleep.[41] Nancel is quick to point out how this unbalanced approach led directly to his contracting a serious eye-disease which in turn slowed down the pace of his studies.

Finally, we may also understand Nancel's discussion of Ramus's irascibility and his tendency to violent rage in terms of the last of the six non-naturals: the passions of the soul. Nancel refers in several places to Ramus's susceptibility to violent anger. Nancel confesses that his own friendship with Ramus was not free from angry outbursts. On the issue of the authorship of Talon's *Rhetoric*, which Ramus published as his own after his collaborator's death, Nancel writes that he was afraid to seek clarification from such an irascible man.[42] Nancel's reluctance may well have been justified, for the passion of anger seems to have afflicted Ramus particularly severely in his relations with his close associates and friends.[43] While Ramus was able to bear attacks from his external enemies in calm silence, when it came to his own colleagues and students he could be not only bad-tempered but also physically brutal. Still, Ramus's fits of rage could be useful, as when, with his own hands, he defended the Collège de Presles from an armed ruffian. Certainly, Nancel declares his intention to furnish the reader of the *Vita Rami* with a straightforward account of his subject without flattery or dissimulation, in line with Plutarch's approach in his *Parallel Lives*.[44] On the other hand, anger was one of the passions of the soul which practitioners of Galenic medicine urged their patients to moderate in the pursuit of health. The best way to do so, they generally argued, was to keep a mirror to hand. To look at one's own reflection, when one's features were grotesquely distorted with rage, would automatically check the onslaught of this passion. As it happens, Nancel indicates that Ramus was accustomed to practise such self-observation, although this was in pursuit of perfect oratorical delivery. Nancel recounts how, when reading at home, Ramus used to gaze at his reflection in a large hemispherical mirror with a green frame and decide how best to compose his features.[45]

In his discussion of the non-naturals in the *Vita Rami*, Nancel continually stresses how Ramus's moderate behaviour in regard to these things formed part of a regular programme, designed expressly to keep him in good health.[46] Nancel credits this regimen, as well as Ramus's good birth and his natural temperance, with his enjoyment of overall good health.[47]

The Galenic non-naturals were thus extremely productive as the terms of reference Nancel uses to generate the material for his portrait of Ramus's daily life. Despite this evident engagement with medical learning, Nancel does not obviously present himself as a learned physician in the *Vita Rami*, apart from his occasional citation of medical authorities, such as, for example, Hippocrates. Nancel's apparent reluctance to adopt an overtly medical persona in the biography is all the more striking as there are several episodes in the text where he might justifiably have presented his learned opinion as a medical practitioner. In particular, as mentioned above, early on in the biography we learn that when Ramus was still a student at the Collège de Navarre his habit of reading late into the night caused his eyes to become painfully inflamed. Nancel relates how Ramus consulted the distinguished physician Jacques Dubois (1478–1555). After a disastrous first attempt at a cure — Dubois advised rest, as well as a pint of good quality wine, a prescription he found in Hippocrates, *Aphorisms* (6.31) — Ramus became temporarily blinded. As a consequence of this bad reaction, Dubois altered his recommended course of treatment, though Nancel does not reveal how. Successfully cured, Ramus went on to pen his most important works. We know from Nancel's other writings that he admired Dubois, like himself a follower of Galen.[48] Such was Nancel's esteem for Dubois's 'authority and originality', that Nancel saw no need to critically annotate his works, as he did those of most other physicians, both ancient and modern.[49] Perhaps Nancel's failure to weigh in as a fellow physician on Dubois's treatment of Ramus in the *Vita Rami* stemmed from his respect for a distinguished colleague's professional judgement.

It is not clear, though, from Nancel's account, how much Dubois contributed to Ramus's eventual cure, and the extent of Ramus's own responsibility for his return to health. As Nancel later reveals, Ramus cut off his hair to save his eyes, which was what, in the end, proved a salutary cure. By including this epilogue in his presentation of Ramus's eye disease and its cure, Nancel tacitly corroborates the contemporary medical view that the physician was not ultimately in control of his patient's health. It was finally the patient who had his health, like his spiritual destiny, in his control.[50] Thus, although Nancel would seem to have eradicated all traces of his perspective as a trained physician from this account of Ramus's eye disease, first by omitting any professional commentary on Dubois's approach and second by highlighting the patient's own role in his ultimate cure, this could not be farther from the truth.

The same anti-interventionist attitude underpins a further episode of illness which we find later on in the *Vita*. Nancel relates how he was present when Ramus suffered an attack of fainting upon trying to remove a ring from his swollen finger. Nancel did not attempt to revive Ramus by administering any remedy, but instead simply remained alone with him for half an hour until he eventually recovered consciousness on his own.[51] Again, Nancel's passivity is typical of contemporary Galenic medicine. Of course, the young Nancel who witnessed Ramus's collapse had not yet begun his professional medical education. Still, in recollecting the episode with the hindsight of a learned physician of twenty years' clinical experience, Nancel could have been pleased at the way in which it announced his fine medical instincts. He certainly had no cause to regret his inaction, which was happily in line with the contemporary medical orthodoxy. Hence, we may conjecture, his inclusion of this rather peculiar and apparently inessential incident in Ramus's life.

Physiognomy in the *Vita Rami*

At precisely the midpoint of the *Vita* (pp. 226–28), Nancel sets a characteristically vivid, finely observed literary portrait of Ramus's 'stature, appearance, natural proportions, and other bodily characteristics; his walk and the gravity of his speech'.[52] The passage precedes the discussion of his 'régime de vie' (pp. 228–40) and moral character (pp. 246–48) I have just been analysing. Like the account of Ramus's diet and general habits, Nancel's elaborate physical description of Ramus is without precedent in the examples of biography discussed thus far. It is indeed curious that in the *Lives* of Budé and Pibrac, we should find no physical description of the subject.[53] Each of their biographers would have been able to supply such information owing to their personal knowledge of their subjects. Whereas Binet does include a thumbnail sketch of Ronsard as a handsome young courtier, he seems to have modelled his description on the engraved portrait of the poet in the *Amours de Cassandre* (1552).[54] The conventional features Binet describes do not suggest any close personal observation of his subject in his old age, when biographer and subject were acquainted. Binet does, however, link Ronsard's features with aspects of his character: with his tranquil brow and gentle, serious eyes, he was the iconic figure of a national poet, 'noble, liberal et vrayment François'.

I would argue that the degree of elaboration we find in Nancel's portrait of Ramus suggests his close familiarity, as a learned physician, with medical theories of physiognomy according to which physical characteristics indicated moral and psychological qualities. Although Nancel did not explicitly link character and countenance in this passage, a physiognomically informed reading of his literary portrait of the philosopher shows that Ramus's features strongly suggest his underlying psychology, as it is depicted by Nancel elsewhere in the text. Since Renaissance doctors widely believed the physiognomists' theories to have a role in diagnosing illness, as a physician, Nancel's direct knowledge of this science is highly probable. None of the works of the ancient or modern physiognomists appear in the catalogue of Nancel's books provided by Sharratt.[55] Still, the idea that the body, as the instrument of the soul, also reflected its qualities was endorsed by none other than Galen himself.[56] Moreover, the rediscovered works of the ancient physiognomists enjoyed tremendous popularity during the sixteenth century and formed part of the university medical curriculum.[57] For example, an early selection of ancient writings on physiognomy, Pietro d'Albano's *Liber compilationis physiognomiæ* (1474) was widely used for teaching purposes by university medical faculties. Perhaps the two most frequently reprinted handbooks of physiognomy in Nancel's day were the French epitome of Bartolomeo della Rocca's Latin text, the *Compendion et brief enseignement de Physiognomie et Chiromancie* (1546), complete with rough woodcut illustrations,[58] and Giovanni Battista della Porta's even more lavishly illustrated *De humana physiognomia* (1586).[59] In the preface of Porta's work, its author advertised medicine as being one of the primary applications of physiognomy.[60] According to Porta, a patient's appearance might furnish the physician with valuable clues about his or her underlying physical weaknesses. Finally, the only contemporary biographer whose texts contain physiognomically informed depictions of physical appearance with anything like the detail found in Nancel's was another medical man, Paolo Giovio (1483–1552).

It is true, though, that the application of physiognomical theories was not limited to learned medicine. In antiquity, biographers like Suetonius and Plutarch exploited the works of physiognomists to describe external aspect in ways which reinforced their overall representation of character.[61] Writers of rhetorical treatises dealing with the rules for encomia and vituperation also advocated its utility for conveying character, facilitating the biographers' adoption of this science. A number of sixteenth-century biographers continued to use physiognomy more or less explicitly in their depictions of physical appearance as Giovio did.[62] So Nancel's recourse to physiognomy, should we choose to see this as underlying his portrait of Ramus, need not have stemmed exclusively from his medical formation. Nancel was also writing in dialogue with the rhetorical traditions of biography.[63]

Before examining Nancel's portrait of Ramus in closer detail, I shall first outline those aspects of physique which the physiognomists considered especially important for the interpretation of character. The writers of treatises on physiognomy did not, however, restrict themselves to analysis of individual features. On the contrary, they tended to discuss features in groups, ascribing certain congeries of features to a particular type of person, such as the magnanimous or the cunning character. Porta in particular used physiognomy to establish a certain number of human typologies. Thus, in his preface to the *De humana physiognomonia*, he stresses physiognomy's utility in determining intellectual aptitudes. In particular, he cited the example of Socrates, who, before agreeing to take on a new student, examined his face to determine his suitability for the study of philosophy.[64] The final book of Porta's work comprises a series of case studies of different types of people characterized by certain combinations of features. The intellectual type, for example, was exemplified by the Italian humanist Pico della Mirandola (1463–94).[65] With this theoretical framework in place, we can then set about interpreting Nancel's portrait physiognomically, both as a device of individual characterization and as a means of advertising Ramus's membership of a certain typology. Of course, it is impossible to determine a single, direct source among the physiognomists' works for each detail of the physical description in the *Vita Rami*. What can be argued with rather more plausibility, however, is the extent to which the features Nancel selected for comment, and the range of terms which he used to describe them, depended on this literature, as well as on the underlying assumption that knowledge of the subject's physical appearance was a matter of more than idle curiosity to the student of character.

Taking Della Rocca and Porta as representative examples, one finds that these writers organized their treatises in chapters that treat individual parts of the body and their associated physical phenomena. They gave the greatest attention to the head and face, and devoted specific chapters to the forehead, eyes, nose, ears, mouth, lips, teeth, tongue, chin and neck. Both Cocles and Porta discussed hair, beard and eyebrows in terms of their colour, texture and quantity. In addition to taking the features separately, Cocles and Porta, following their classical predecessors, also considered the overall proportions of the body.[66] For instance, they deemed a well-proportioned body to be characteristic of men who were brave and upright in a moral sense, as well as gentle and affectionate with their comrades. Besides the individual parts of the body and its overall proportions, the breath, laughter, tone of voice, and gait were also important physiognomic indicators of character.

With Della Rocca's and Porta's works in mind, we can now proceed to analyse Nancel's portrait of Ramus in physiognomic terms. First, Nancel comments on his subject's height, posture and overall proportions:

> Ramus was a tall man, a little above normal height, upright and distinguished, rather thick-set and solidly built, and well-proportioned in each and every part of the body.[67]

Porta associated the tall, upright physique Nancel described here with a brave and irascible ('iracundus') character.[68] According to Porta, one should expect a man with such a figure to be bellicose and audacious, since the shape of his body recalled that of a spear. An erect posture was also a sign of a clever person ('vir ingeniosus'). Intellectual ability, but also, as we have seen, irascibility were both characteristic of Ramus in Nancel's estimation. Nancel specifically terms Ramus 'iracundus' and notes that his students were terrified of his notorious fits of brutality.[69] Audacity, too, is equally consistent with Nancel's more general characterization of his subject in the *Vita Rami*. For instance, Ramus's courage in the face of physical danger emerges not only from Nancel's account of his tragic martyrdom, but also from an earlier episode, mentioned above, in which Ramus caught and flogged an armed intruder in the Collège de Presles.[70]

The next element in Nancel's portrait is Ramus's colouring: 'his skin was darkish ('subfusco'), not so much black as not quite white enough for a Frenchman'.[71] Porta, in his remarks on complexion, associated both extremes of pallor and darkness with the negative qualities of effeminacy, timidity, and voluptuousness.[72] Porta therefore situated the complexion indicating fortitude somewhere in between, just as Nancel described Ramus's colouring. Porta terms this middle colour 'fuscus', which finds an echo in Nancel's 'subfusco'. Interpreted physiognomically, then, Ramus's colouring would identify him as brave and fearless. At the same time, such fortitude (*fortitudo*) was another of Cicero's *habitus laudabiles*.

Nancel next comments that Ramus had a large head, a feature which Porta illustrates by comparison with a dog.[73] Physiognomists typically supposed people with amply-sized heads to be, like the canines they resembled, acutely perceptive and of keen intellect, in addition to being brave and magnanimous. Ramus's hair was black and his beard 'thick, black, bushy, full and flowing'. Although Porta as a general rule associates the colour black with timidity, he qualifies his judgement by adding that, in hair, it might also indicate a cunning nature.[74] To the physiognomically informed reader, then, Ramus's dark locks could connote his resourceful mind. Physiognomically speaking, his bushy beard is likewise a positive sign, indicating a good nature.[75]

As for the colour of Ramus's eyes, Nancel describes them as dark but, more significantly, bright ('charops'). Referring to the pertinent chapter in Porta, we find that such eyes are yet another characteristic of the intellectual type ('vir ingeniosus').[76] But it was not just the clever man whose eyes were typically 'charops'. Porta also offered an extended definition of this colour, which he identifies as being the same as that of lions' and eagles' eyes. Porta claims that those with this eye colour should therefore have the courage and spirit of these beasts. Similarly, Porta associates an aquiline nose like Ramus's with a regal, magnanimous character, as the eagle was the mythical ancestor of kings.[77] Although Nancel extols his subject's humble origins at the beginning of the *Vita Rami*,[78] he repeatedly insists on Ramus's regal dignity and aptitude for governance, alleging this as the reason Ramus, and not his colleagues Omer Talon or Barthélemy Alexandre, became the principal first of the Marian College and later of the Collège de Presles.[79]

Ramus's belly, which Nancel describes as protruding, is more problematic in terms of his physical characterization as an intellectual and a courageous leader. In physiognomic theory, a distended stomach portended multifarious vices, from intellectual sluggishness and stolidity to pride and voluptuousness.[80] Indeed, Porta cites the proverbial expression that the stomach was fed at the expense of the intellect.[81] In order not to compromise his portrait of Ramus as an intellectual, Nancel therefore specifies that Ramus's paunch was only slightly rounded ('paulum prominulo').

Finally, after having attended to Ramus's physical aspect, Nancel describes the philosopher's customary facial expression ('frank and open with the lips almost always slightly apart') and his dignified, grave, indeed regal, manner of walking. Nancel also noted the sound of Ramus's voice, which he classifies as between bass and tenor, yet sonorous and pleasant to listen to.[82] This is, for Porta, the best kind of voice, and it signifies both audacity and eloquence, two of the most salient and praiseworthy qualities Nancel attributes to Ramus, the most brilliant of orators.[83] But Nancel proceeds to qualify his first statement about Ramus's voice, which, he adds, underwent a significant modulation whilst lecturing:

> When, however, he raised his voice in his teaching, then it became softer (*gracilescebat*), especially when he repeated frequently as he did, 'Therefore, therefore'.[84]

Interestingly, Porta reminds his reader that both Plato's and Aristotle's voices tended to be soft ('gracilis'), exactly as Nancel describes Ramus's lecturing voice. In general, though, such a gentle voice was a physiognomic indicator of a peaceful, modest soul and a blameless moral character.[85]

Taken as a whole, then, Ramus's features, as Nancel describes them in this passage, reinforce his overall characterization of him as a man of pre-eminent intellectual and moral qualities. But it is clear both from a physiognomic reading of this portrait, and from a number of other anecdotes in the *Vita*, that physical bravery, in addition to, as we have already seen, violence, were also noteworthy aspects of his character. Besides being a scholar, Nancel's Ramus is a leader of men. It is thus not incongruous that the principal of the Collège de Presles should have some of the aquiline and leonine traits that physiognomists associated with kings. As one would expect, though, when assessed as a composite portrait, Nancel's depiction of Ramus's individual features is most strongly reminiscent of Porta's picture of the man devoted to the study of the liberal arts.[86]

Conclusion: Galen and Nancel

I have been arguing that learned medicine was an informing discourse in the *Vita Rami*. Nancel does not identify himself explicitly as a professional physician in this work, but he uses his theoretical knowledge of Galenic notions of regimen to recreate Ramus's daily life at a distance of twenty years. The importance of moderation in the Galenic conception of health similarly shapes his portrayal of Ramus's moral character. Nancel gears his depiction of the philosopher to show him always striving to embrace the middle way. At the same time, this conforms to canons of epideictic rhetoric — the branch to which biography belonged — which identified temperance as a cardinal virtue. Ramus's countenance, to the physiognomically informed reader, is at the same time that of an intellectual and a brave leader. Such fortitude likewise belonged to the Ciceronian constellation of dispositions worthy of the orator's praise.

To understand Nancel's motivations in writing the *Vita*, it is necessary to consider another of his works where his adoption of a medical persona is closer to the surface. In a fascinating descriptive catalogue of his own works that he published in 1603, Nancel identifies himself with Galen both in his self-presentation and in his authorial attitude. Nancel claims to have taken his cue from Galen, whom he called his 'præceptor' in medicine, in publishing a catalogue of his own books.[87] The Galenic example may also be behind Nancel's display of intellectual versatility. As this *Catalogus* attests, Nancel was indeed a polymath, a prolific writer in both prose and verse on a great range of subjects who, in addition to his *Vita Rami*, produced philological commentaries on various Greek and Latin writers from Aristotle to Cicero and Vergil, works on mathematics and theology, as well as medical treatises.[88] Galen too had written voluminously not only on medical topics such as anatomy and physiology, but also on logic and moral philosophy as well as compiling philological studies of both medical and non-medical authors. Moreover, Galen considered intellectual training in non-medical topics critical to the formation of the best doctors.[89] Galen's inquiring mind and his prodigious appetite for intellectual labour were at the heart of his, admittedly self-based, description of the ideal physician.[90]

In his *Catalogus*, Nancel too presents himself as exceptionally devoted to the life of the mind. Even after he had completed his formal university education, as a young man, Nancel made clear that he had continued to engage in private study as an independent scholar. When not travelling and at home, he claimed, scarcely a day had gone by over the past thirty-five years in which he had not read and written for at least ten hours, and often even twelve or fifteen. Nancel engaged in this dogged pursuit of knowledge despite his awareness that his was an 'unhappy age, in which little, not to say no, honour accrues to virtue, learning or scholarship'.[91] The people of his time, writes Nancel in his *Catalogus*, were more intent on 'pursuing the pleasure of the ears, and even more so of the table, or of sex' than on dedicating themselves to the comparatively arid occupations of reading or writing. Both ordinary and prominent folk alike all too readily cast aside study in favour of the sensual titillation afforded by 'the crackling of the fire in the hearth, the banging of pans in the kitchen, the cries of the stage and the theatre, and games and jokes'. Nancel's castigation of his morally degenerate age in which the overriding concern was with pleasure evokes a parallel with the similar diatribes of his illustrious medical forebear, Galen. The shameful tendency of Galen's contemporaries to reject the austere pursuit of the truth in order to indulge in 'dicing, sexual encounters, bathing, drinking, carousing and other sensual pleasures' was a stock Galenic theme.[92] Anyone who, like Galen himself, abstained from such dissolute behaviour to spend their time in study was, that author declared, more likely to be thought mad than to be honoured.

But abstemiousness and scholarly industry were nonetheless the two qualities Galen stipulated to be preconditions for success in the physician, as he made abundantly clear in *The best doctor is also a philosopher.* The true doctor must be hard-working and one cannot be hard-working if one is continually drinking, eating or excessively addicted to sex: 'in short a slave to belly and genitals'.[93] So Nancel, both in his censorious authorial stance and in his self-presentation as a hard-working universal scholar in the *Catalogus* conforms to the Galenic ideal for the professional doctor.

Unlike Galen, though, who generally claimed that he published his works only unwillingly in order to ensure that they did not circulate in unauthorized, pirated versions, Nancel was extraordinarily determined — one might even say, obsessed — that the fruits of his intellectual labours should 'see the much desired light of day'. The reason behind his contempt for his morally degenerate age becomes apparent when we discover in Nancel's *Catalogus* how he had scoured the whole of France, mostly in vain, in order to find a publisher for his many works. He relates with more than a tinge of bitterness how the malicious rivalry of some Parisian doctors and the absence of a scholarly public largely doomed these attempts at publication in his native France to failure.[94] Having exhausted this avenue, Nancel next turned his attention to Italy and to Germany — after all, the home of printing — in the hopes of attracting the attention of a publisher. Despite his efforts, he reluctantly conceded that much of his work was destined for 'only the murky darkness in which it is now skulking'.[95]

Nancel's account in the *Catalogus* of his difficulties in finding an outlet in print for his vast scholarly production is, like the *Vita Rami*, strikingly confessional in tenor. For Nancel, writing about the self seems to have had a compulsive quality. Citing Jerome as his model, Nancel declares that his was a life bound up with his writing.[96] He did own, though, that his Herculean rhythm of work was interrupted by many hours and days 'squandered without writing a line'. Nancel admits to spending this time off 'indulging in witty games and pastimes'. Ever the conscientious physician, however, Nancel consecrated his leisure moments to 'looking after bodily health and wellbeing', both his own and that of his patients.[97] Still, Nancel was distressed by the fact that, because this time went unrecorded in his writing, no trace of it remained for posterity. In the *Catalogus*, Nancel imagines a critic who might ask him why he had gone to such efforts to provide a list of his unpublished works, both those completed and those in preparation. His reply is that he wished not only to 'exhort and incite the younger generation to equal if not greater industriousness', but also to provide his reader with an account of the life he had led 'in the sight of God and the angels'.[98] It is as if Nancel required the medium of print to validate his existence.

The *Catalogus*, then, with its account of simultaneous yearning for public exposure and difficulty achieving publication, provides us with some important context that enables us to understand the functional utility of the biography of Ramus for Nancel. The pretext for writing the *Vita Rami* was Nancel's desire to express his gratitude to his teacher, although he admits, citing proverbial wisdom and Aristotle, that it was impossible to repay a teacher satisfactorily. Nancel's acknowledgement of his debt to his teacher invites us to understand the writing of biography as a negotiation in the world. Addressing himself to the pan-European community of all former students of Ramus, Nancel obligingly asserts that they shone out like brilliant lights in the contemporary scholarly firmament. Even more significantly, by their learned publications, they were handing their names to future generations. We may view the *Vita Rami*, then, as an ideal platform from which Nancel might assert his own intellectual ambitions, and possibly also pave the way for the publication of more of his own works. Indeed, the *Vita*, although it sometimes appears as a separate volume, was originally published together with a book of Nancel's own speeches, one of which was an apology for medicine.[99] Writing and publishing the biography of an established — though not uncontroversial — scholar such as the Professor of Eloquence and Philosophy at the Collège royal (1551–72) allowed Nancel to both identify himself with his master and seek the entry into the scholarly community he so desperately craved.

Notes to Chapter 4

1. Nicolas de Nancel, *Petri Rami Vita* (Paris: Claude Morel, 1600 [1599]) (=*VR*). Further references to this text are to the edition with English translation in Peter Sharratt, 'Nicolaus Nancelius, *Petri Rami Vita*, edited with an English Translation', *Humanistica Lovaniensia* 24 (1975), 161–277.
2. See, for example, the author of the anonymous *Régime de vivre, et conservation du corps humain* (Paris: Vincent Sertenas, 1561) who suggested washing the head with a fragrant decoction of wine, rosemary and sage in the winter and essences of rose and myrtle in summer (fol. 6v°).
3. *VR*, p. 262–63 and 266–72. In a further gesture attenuating confessional differences, Nancel sought to portray Ramus as one whose chief concern was the concord of all Christians. *VR*, p. 260.
4. *VR*, p. 186.
5. *VR*, p. 194.
6. See Marie-Dominique Couzinet and Jean-Marc Mandosio, 'Nouveaux éclairages sur les cours de Ramus et de ses collègues au collège de Presles d'après des notes inédites prises par Nancel', in *Ramus et l'Université* (Paris: Presses de l'ENS, 2004), pp. 11–48.
7. *VR*, p. 244.
8. See Georges Cardon, *La Fondation de l'université de Douai* (Paris: Alcan, 1892), pp. 410–16. Although, as a Catholic, Nancel did not need to flee Paris in the early 1560s, his position at Presles would have become insecure when his mentor Ramus left the city in 1562.
9. Cardon, *La Fondation*, p. 417.
10. Sharratt, 'Nicolas de Nancel (1539–1610)', in *Acta Conventus Neo-Latini Amsteldamensis* (Munich, 1979), pp. 918–27 (p. 918).
11. Sharratt, 'Nicolas de Nancel: A Medical and Theological View of the Other Sex', in *Female*

Saints and Sinners: Saintes et Mondaines (France 1450–1650), ed. by Jennifer Britnell and Ann Moss (Durham: University of Durham, 2002), pp. 109–21.

12. Sharratt, 'Nicolas Nancelius', p. 165.
13. For a complete picture of Nancel's medical erudition, see Sharratt 'The Lost Library of Nicolas de Nancel', *History of Universities*, 19.2 (2004), pp. 1–90 (pp. 48–80).
14. Sharratt, 'Nicolas de Nancel', p. 922.
15. Nancy Siraisi, *The Clock and the Mirror: Girolamo Cardano and Renaissance Medicine* (Princeton, NJ: Princeton University Press, 1997), p. 15 and p. 19. On the shift towards direct observation in later medieval medicine, see Michael R. McVaugh, 'Bedside Manners in the Middle Ages', *Bulletin of the History of Medicine*, 71 (1997), 201–23.
16. Paraphrased from Mariano Santo (*c.*1488–1564), pioneer of lithotomy, the surgical intervention for kidney stones. Siraisi, 'Medicine, Physiology and Anatomy in Early Sixteenth-Century Critiques of the Arts and the Sciences', in *New Perspectives on Renaissance Thought: Essays in the History of Science, Education and Philosophy in Memory of Charles B. Schmitt*, ed. by John Henry and Sarah Hutton (London: Duckworth, 1990), pp. 214–19 (p. 225). Cited by Ian Maclean, *Logic, Signs and Nature in the Renaissance: The Case of Learned Medicine* (Cambridge: Cambridge University Press, 2002), p. 79. On Nancel's attitude to experiment and method, see Sharratt, 'Nicolas de Nancel: A Medical and Theological View of the Other Sex', pp. 117–18.
17. '[...] iis qui non viderunt, nec audierunt, ipse qui vidi, audivi, pernovi, indico, insinuo, indigito; et quidem quantum recordari queo, quam tum per annos prope viginti contubernalis observari [...]' *VR*, p. 170.
18. 'Experientia quidem artem genuit, inexperientia autem temeritatem ... [ut] nullum in artibus documentum recipiendum, quod ab usu et experientia verorum exemplorum observatum et inductum non esset'. *Scholæ in Liberales Artes*, col. 830. Cited in James Veazie Skalnik, *Ramus and Reform: University and Church at the End of the Renaissance*, Sixteenth Century essays and studies, 60 (Kirksville, MO: Truman State University Press, 2002), p. 49. Although scholars such as Hooykaas have seen in Ramus the link between literary and scientific empiricism, Skalnik cautions against identifying Ramus's method with the 'scientific empiricism' of later eras, since Ramist induction is made from literary works and not from nature. Reijer Hooykaas, 'Pierre de la Ramée et l'empirisme scientifique au XVIe siècle', in *La Science au seizième siècle: Colloque international Royaumont, 1–4 juillet 1957* (Paris: Hermann, 1960), pp. 297–311.
19. Compare the brief section (fols. b1–b2) on physical appearance and regimen in Théophile de Banos, *P. Rami vita*, in Petrus Ramus, *Commentariorum de religione christiana libri quatuor, nunquam antea editi: eiusdem vita, a Theophilo Banosio descripta* (Frankfurt: A. Wechel, 1576), fols. a1–c4. Even more sparing are the conventional portraits in Jean-Jacques Boissard, 'Petrus Ramus', in *Icones uirorum illustrium, doctrina et eruditione præstantium..., II. Pars* (Frankfurt: Théodore De Bry, 1592), pp. 96–103; and Jean Thomas Freige, *Petri Rami vita*, in Petrus Ramus, *Prælectiones in Ciceronis orationes octo consulares* (Basel: J. Perna, 1575), pp. 5–46 (see p. 9).
20. For discussions of the significance of this episode within Montaigne's 'essai', see, for example, John O'Brien, 'At Montaigne's Table', *French Studies*, 54.1 (2000), 1–16; Jean Céard, 'La Culture du corps: Montaigne et la diététique de son temps', in *Le Parcours des Essais: Montaigne 1588–1988*, ed. by Marcel Tetel and G. Mallory Masters (Paris: Aux Amateurs des Livres, 1989), pp. 83–96; and Jules Brody, *Lectures de Montaigne* (Lexington, KY: French Forum, 1982), pp. 67–92.
21. Céard, 'La Culture du corps', p. 84.
22. Céard, 'La Culture du corps', pp. 88–89. *Régime de vivre*, fol. 17v°.
23. Galen, 'To Thrasyboulos: is healthiness a part of medicine or gymnastics?', in *Selected Works*, trans. by P. N. Singer (Oxford, 1997), pp. 67–68; 'The Art of medicine', in ibid., p. 374. Galen, 'On the Preservation of Health' (1.15.5–9) presents a quadruple classification: those things which are consumed; those things which are eliminated; those things which are applied or performed; those things which take place in the surroundings. Luis García Ballester, 'On the Origin of the "Six Non-natural Things" in Galen', *Galen und das hellenistische Erbe. Verhandlungen des IV. Internationalen Galen-Symposiums*, ed. by J. Kollesch and D. Nickel (Stuttgart: Franz Steiner, 1993), pp. 105–15.
24. Lawrence Brockliss and Colin Jones, *The Medical World of Early Modern France* (Oxford: Clarendon Press, 1997), p. 112.

25. Galen, 'An Exhortation to Study the Arts', in *Selected Works*, p. 47.
26. Galen, 'The Art of medicine', in *Selected Works*, p. 374. Brockliss and Jones, *Medical World*, p. 115.
27. Cicero, *De inventione*, 2.153.159–63.
28. *VR*, p. 230.
29. *Regime de vivre*, fols. 35r°–36v° and fols. 62 r°–v°.
30. *Regime de vivre*, fol. 9r°.
31. *VR*, pp. 232–34.
32. *Regime de vivre*, fol. 8v°.
33. Céard, 'La Diététique dans la médicine de la Renaissance', in *Pratiques et discours alimentaires à la Renaissance*, ed. by J. C. Margolin and R. Sauzet (Paris: Maissonneuve & Larose, 1982), pp. 20–36.
34. *VR*, p. 240.
35. *Régime de vivre*, fols. 5–6; Nicolas-Abraham de La Framboisière, *Gouvernement nécessaire à chacun pour vivre longuement en santé* (Paris: Michel Sonnius, 1601), p. 139 : 'Les yeux sont pareillement occupez à regarder le mouvement de la bale, et l'esprit continuellement bandé à espier l'occasion de joüer, pour gaigner en fin le prix, et emporter l'honneur'.
36. *De l'utilité qui provient du jeu de paume au corps et à l'esprit*, trans. by Forbet L'Aisné (Paris: T. Sevestre, 1599).
37. *VR*, p. 244.
38. *VR*, p. 236.
39. *VR*, p. 230. This was not ideal, according to the 1561 *Regime de vivre*, but if the habit of a post-prandial siesta proved impossible to break, it could be permitted in the dog days of summer (p. 10).
40. *VR*, p. 236.
41. *VR*, p. 178.
42. *VR*, p. 218.
43. *VR*, p. 246.
44. *VR*, p. 170 and p. 252.
45. *VR*, p. 228.
46. *VR*, p. 236.
47. *VR*, p. 240.
48. Nancel, 'Catalogus librorum ab auctore scriptorum', in *Nic Nancelii...Epistolarum de pluribus reliquarum...Eiusdem præfationes in Novum Testamentum* (Paris: Claude Morel, 1603), pp. 124–55. I cite this text in the edition with translation and notes in Sharratt, 'The Lost Library of Nicolas de Nancel', pp. 4–43. Nancel's reference to Dubois is on page 17.
49. Nancel, 'Catalogus', p. 17.
50. Brockliss and Jones, *Medical World*, p. 116; David E. Linden, 'Gabriele de Zerbi's *De cautelis medicorum* and the Tradition of Medical Prudence', *Bulletin of the History of Medicine*, 73 (1999), 19–37 (pp. 31–32).
51. *VR*, p. 240.
52. *VR*, pp. 226–28. No engraving of Ramus accompanies the text of his biography, but the *Testamentum Petri Rami* (1576) bears one.
53. As mentioned in ch. 2 above, a portrait engraving of Pibrac adorned Guy du Faur d'Hermay's translation of Paschal's *Pibrachii Vita*.
54. '[Il avoit] le visage noble, liberal et vrayment François, la barbe blondoyante, cheveux chastains, nez aquilin, les yeux pleins de douce gravité, et le front serein' (*Vie de Ronsard*, 9). See Patricia Eichel-Lojkine, *Le Siècle des grands hommes: Les Recueils de vies d'hommes illustres au XVIème siècle* (Louvain and Sterling, VA: Peeters, 2001), p. 121. On this engraving of Ronsard, see Malcolm Quainton, 'The Liminary Texts of Ronsard's *Amours de Cassandre* (1552): Poetics, Erotics, Semiotics', *French Studies*, 53.3 (1999), 257–78 (pp. 265–71).
55. Sharratt, 'Lost Library', pp. 48–80.
56. See Galen, 'The soul's dependence on the body', in *Selected Works*, pp. 163–64 and 'The usefulness of the parts' (Kühn 3.2–3). Galen followed (pseudo-)Aristotle, *Physiognomica*, in the view that physical characteristics might furnish the physician with valuable indications of

character, although he cautioned against the reductive application of physiognomical precepts. In his estimation, these were limited in usefulness since they did not address causes. Hairy thighs might connote lust in men, but they did not explain it.

57. Besides editions of Adamantius, pseudo-Aristotle and Polemo, numerous derivative contemporary works ensured the transmission of the ancient art of physiognomy. The following is a selective list of such works: Michel Angelo Biondo, *De cognitione hominis per aspectum* (Rome: A. Bladum, 1544); Jean de Indagine, *Introductiones apotelesmaticæ elegantes, in Chyromantiam, Physiognomiam ...*, (Frankfurt: D. Zephelius, 1522), Translation by Antoine Du Moulin: *Chiromance et physiognomie* (Lyons: Jean de Tournes, 1549). Du Moulin himself authored several physiognomical handbooks: *De diversa hominum natura* (Lyons: Jean de Tournes, 1549); and *Physionomie naturelle* (Lyons: Jean de Tournes, 1550). Paolo Pinzio, *Fisionomia* (Lyons: Jean de Tournes, 1550).
58. The Latin original was first published in Bologna in 1504. The French epitome went through numerous editions during the sixteenth century and was even reissued as late as the end of the seventeenth. I quote from P. Drouart's 1546 Paris edition.
59. Vico Equense: Giuseppe Cacchi, 1586. I quote from Naples: Tarquinio Longo, 1602. There was also an Italian translation of this work (first edition, Napoli: G. G. Carlino & C. Vitale, 1610; I quote from Vicenza: P. Tozzi, 1615).
60. *Physiognomonia*, p. 3.
61. Eichel-Lojkine, *Le Siècle des grands hommes*, pp. 113–15; E. C. Evans 'Roman Descriptions of Personal Appearance in History and Biography', *Harvard Studies in Classical Philology* 46 (1935), 43–84.
62. The use of physiognomy to interpret physical characteristics is most notable amongst humanist writers in Latin, for example, in Erasmus's epistolary biography of Thomas More (Allen, IV, 12–23) and in Beatus Rhenanus's portrait of Erasmus which recycled Erasmus's own description of More (Allen, I, 70; Allen, IV, 14 notices the similarity).
63. On Nancel's reliance on canons of epideictic rhetoric derived from Aphthonius and others, see Kees Meerhoff, *Rhétorique et poétique au XVIe siècle en France. Du Bellay, Ramus et les autres* (Leiden: Brill, 1986), p. 318 and notes 9, 10.
64. *Physiognomonia*, fol. 2.
65. *Physiognomonia*, fol. 237. In the Italian translation of this work, Porta claimed, without wishing to be seen to boast, that his own figure, which he went on to describe, resembled that of the intellectual (*Fisonomia*, fol. 181 v°).
66. Evans, 'Roman Descriptions', pp. 64–74.
67. 'Ramus statura corporis fuit procera, et quam mediocris, paulo celsiore, recta et eleganti, satis densa solidaque, bene ad proportionem partium universarum singularumque compositi [*sic* — for 'composita' ?]'. *VR*, pp. 226–28.
68. *Physiognomonia*, fol. 209.
69. *VR*, p. 246.
70. *VR*, p. 246.
71. 'colore subfusco, et non tam nigro, quam minime albo [...]' *VR*, p. 246.
72. *Physiognomonia*, fol. 197.
73. *Physiognomonia*, fol. 50.
74. *Physiognomonia*, fol. 228.
75. Della Rocca, *Compendion*, fol. b 6v°. Nancel describes how Ramus deliberately grew his beard to enhance his dignity and philosophical appearance (*VR*, p. 240). When ordered to shave by the Rector, Ramus refused to show himself outside for some time due to embarrassment. Nancel thus portrays Ramus as being self-consciously aware of his own image and his power to manipulate it.
76. *Physiognomonia*, fols. 173–74.
77. *Physiognomonia*, fols. 76–77.
78. *VR*, pp. 172–74.
79. *VR*, p. 180 and p. 181.
80. *Physiognomonia*, fols. 130–31.
81. As Galen had cited the proverb 'a fat stomach does not make a fine mind' in 'Is healthiness a part of medicine or gymnastics?', *Selected Works*, p. 88.

82. '(inter basin et tenorem media) sonora tamen, et auditu suavis' (*VR*, p. 228).
83. *Physiognomonia*, fols. 104–08; *VR*, p. 204.
84. 'Nisi quod in docendo siquando efferret altius, jam tum *gracilescebat*, maxime cum illud sibi frequens ingeminaret (ergo, ergo)'. *VR*, p. 228.
85. *Physiognomonia*, fol. 108.
86. *Physiognomonia*, fol. 237.
87. Nancel, *Catalogus*, p. 5. See Galen, 'On my own Books'; 'On the Order of My Own Books'.
88. Only two medical publications resulted from Nancel's scholarship during his lifetime: a *Discours de la Peste* (Paris: Denys du Val, 1581) dedicated to the citizens of Tours and *De legitimo partus tempore*, a contribution to the ongoing debate over that important medico-legal question of the length of pregnancy in the human female (Paris: J. Richerium, 1586). His posthumously published magnum opus, the *Analogia microcosmi ad macrocosmon* (Paris: Claude Morel, 1611) should also be classed amongst his medical works, though.
89. Galen, 'Quod optimus medicus sit quoque philosophus'; 'De constitutione artis medicinæ', ch. 6. Linden, 'Gabriele de Zerbi', pp. 22–23 and p. 30.
90. See, for example, Galen, 'De locis affectis', iii.7 (Kühn 3.167). Maclean, *Logic*, p. 93.
91. Sharratt, 'Lost Library', p. 10.
92. Galen, *On the Therapeutic Method. Books I and II.* Translated with an introduction and commentary by R. J. Hankinson (Oxford: Clarendon Press, 1991), p. 81.
93. Galen, 'The best doctor is also a philosopher', *Selected Works*, p. 33.
94. *Catalogus*, p. 27 and p. 29.
95. *Catalogus*, p. 27.
96. *Catalogus*, p. 5.
97. *Catalogus*, p. 41.
98. *Catalogus*, p. 43.
99. *Nancelii ... Declamationum liber, eas complectens orationes, quas vel ipse juvenis habuit ad populum, vel per discipulos recitavit, tum Lutetiæ olim docens, tum in Academiæ Duacensi regius professor institutus, in quibus præcipua est medicinæ ... apologia et jurisprudentiæ encomium...* (Paris: Claude Morel, 1600 [1599]). Sharratt, 'Nicolaus Nancelius', p. 164.

Figure 5. Portrait of d'Aubigné, 1622. Geneva, Bibliothèque publique universitaire.

CHAPTER 5

Staging Baroque Autobiography: Spectacle in Agrippa d'Aubigné's *Sa Vie à ses enfants* (1629)

Agrippa d'Aubigné (1552–1630), Huguenot, soldier, and man of letters, composed his autobiography, *Sa Vie à ses enfants* in the year before his death.[1] Compiled during his final period of exile in Protestant Geneva, d'Aubigné's autobiography ostensibly scripts his *exit* from the theatre of court life, rather than preparing a glorious entrance to it. As we have already seen, for Le Roy and Paschal, young men needing an entrée into court at the start of their careers, the desire to play a leading role at court underlay their biographical enterprise. With d'Aubigné, the reverse appears at first glance to be the case. *Sa Vie* stages a seemingly unending series of explosive quarrels followed by brief reconciliations between d'Aubigné and his master, the Protestant prince Henri de Navarre (the future King Henri IV), whose religious tergiversations and ultimate conversion to Catholicism so disappointed him.[2] *Sa Vie* certainly does emphasize its author's personal distance, throughout his life, from the theatricality and corruption of the Valois court and more specifically that of his master, Navarre. Whereas Le Roy devoted a significant portion of his biography of Budé to a digression containing an encomium of François I, and Paschal tactfully omitted to mention Charles IX's role in the St. Bartholomew's Day massacres, d'Aubigné frequently vituperates Navarre, whom he presents as a debauched criminal.[3] D'Aubigné further attempts to dissociate himself from the court preoccupation with spectacle by giving only the most cursory treatment of his time at the Valois court in Paris during the 1570s, when, as a poet, he composed *balets de cour* and other similar entertainments.[4]

Despite his apparent repudiation of the theatricality characteristic of contemporary court life, d'Aubigné is at once playwright, 'metteur en scène' and consummate actor in the text of *Sa Vie*. Scholars have generally tended to view d'Aubigné's autobiography as a 'récit parabolique' in which the Calvinist recounts the itinerary of his religious vocation.[5] According to this reading of *Sa Vie*, d'Aubigné would present himself as God's faithful servant who courts martyrdom at every turn.[6] I do not wish to contest the validity of this line of interpretation, but rather to suggest a complementary approach. Instead of exploring the spiritual or ideological message of *Sa Vie*, I wish to examine how d'Aubigné puts his acting and directing abilities to work in the service of the Protestant cause. In *Sa Vie*, d'Aubigné shows how to derive advantage from the theatricality which increasingly governed the courtier's existence under the last of the Valois kings.[7] With his every gesture, he shows his awareness of the importance of audience response. His own reliance on dramatic performance in turn validates these skills as important for the aspiring soldier of the faith to emulate. That d'Aubigné honed these role-playing skills at court suggests the need to reassess the view of his autobiographical persona as one in perpetual conflict with a milieu characterized by the baroque culture of theatricality. It also links d'Aubigné's autobiography with the *Lives* of Budé, Pibrac, Ronsard and Ramus as a text which mediates between individual and collectivity to provide a mechanism by which the younger generation may inscribe itself into the existing cultural framework.

Autobiographers, in narrating their lives, invariably seek to make their texts meaningful by imposing a structure on their account: a key autobiographical concept that Lejeune formulated as 'le désir structurant'.[8] And indeed, as the author of his personal drama, d'Aubigné did not reproduce the years of his life at the time of composing *Sa Vie* on a proportionate number of manuscript pages. While the underlying structure of *Sa Vie* does not possess the dramatic unity expected of a stage play even in the pre-classical era, it does have an episodic quality which owes much to Renaissance spectacle. D'Aubigné narrated important events in a series of discrete scenes or 'tableaux'. In retelling his life to his children, he created dramatic tension by insisting on the shadow of death which hangs over almost every moment.[9] This dramatic tension, which Bouwsma describes as belonging to the pleasure of the theatre, makes d'Aubigné's life narrative compelling reading or listening for his intended audience.[10]

Still, d'Aubigné's brilliant deployment of these theatrical devices in narrating *Sa Vie* stands curiously at odds with his rejection of the empty theatricality of court life throughout his œuvre, typically in autobiographical passages. His epic poem of the civil wars of religion, the *Tragiques*, exemplifies this. D'Aubigné had signed the 1616 first edition of this work 'le Bouc du désert' as a way of signalling the profound antagonism between the poet and his milieu. Numerous episodes in the *Tragiques* involve virulent anti-court satire. For example, the second book, 'Princes' contains an allegorical depiction of the arrival at the Valois court of a young man traditionally identified with d'Aubigné himself.[11] In a dream, Fortune and Virtue impart to him starkly conflicting advice on his conduct in the midst of the general iniquity of the court. Fortune tells the young courtier he must learn to join in the general masquerade by acting an obsequious part:

> [...] assez pour gentil-homme,
> Pour sembler vertueux en peinture, ou bien comme
> Un singe porte en soi quelque chose d'humain
> Aux gestes, au visage, au pied et à la main.[12]

There follows detailed guidance on how to create the role of the courtier in both dress and gesture:

> Il reste que le corps comme l'accoustrement
> Soit aux loix de la cour: marcher mignonnement,

> Trainer les pieds, mener les bras, hocher la teste,
> Pour bransler à propos d'un pennache la creste [...][13]

Virtue intervenes just in time to save the young man from being irredeemably caught up in the degenerate theatre of court life.

D'Aubigné likewise castigated the court for its constant charade in the *Avantures du Baron de Fæneste* (1617–1630), a satirical dialogue between a young Catholic courtier, Fæneste (from the Greek verb φαίνεσθαι meaning 'to appear') and a Protestant gentleman, Enay (from εἶναι, 'to be'). Scholars have identified d'Aubigné with the sober character of Enay, 'vieil Gentilhomme [...] consommé aux lettres, aux experiences de la Cour et de la Guerre', who opposes Fæneste's superficiality and histrionics.[14] Early on in this work, Fæneste delights in telling Enay all about the current court fashions, which are designed to be as ostentatious as possible. Enay then prompts Fæneste to tell him how one makes a properly theatrical entrance at court:

> E. Et bien, voila pour les habillmens: estans ainsi vestu à la trotte qui mode, que faictes-vous aprés pour paroistre? — F. Non pas, non, on descend entre les gardes, entendez: bous commencez à rire au premier que bous rencontrez: bous saluez l'un, bous dittes le mot à l'autre: «*Fraire, que tu es vrave, espanoüy comme une rose, tu es vien traitté de ta maistresse. Cette cruelle, cette revelle, rent-elle point les armes à ce veau front, à ceste moustache vien troussee, et puis ceste velle greve, c'est pour en mourir.*» Il faut dire cela en demenant les vras, vranlant la teste, changeant de pied, peignant d'une men la moustache, et d'aucunefois les chebus.[15]

D'Aubigné also denounced the hypocrisy required of the courtier in a much earlier 'Elégie', written sometime around 1577, in a period of retreat from the court after the peace of Bergerac which put an end to the sixth of the Wars of Religion.[16] This poem, typically referred to by modern editors as the 'Elégie autobiographique', extols the purity of rustic life and lambastes, from first-hand experience, the sycophancy and excesses of the court.

D'Aubigné's overt critique of the court for its theatre of appearances in *Sa Vie* and elsewhere constitutes a vigorous response to a cultural phenomenon Jacqueline Boucher has termed 'la théâtralisation de la vie de cour'.[17] During the final quarter of the sixteenth century, carefully choreographed festivals proliferated to transform every aspect of the life of the court into a performance. So great was the court's appetite for festivals that in 1585, Henri III created the office of 'grand maître de cérémonies' in order to oversee their intricate preparations.[18] In staging these events, Henri III continued a trend begun by Catherine de Médicis, who, during her regency, had exploited festivals in her government of France. Frances Yates has brilliantly analysed how the queen regent used spectacular entertainments, such as tournaments performed in exotic masquerade costumes, to defuse the tensions between Catholic and Protestant by transforming the real conflict into a chivalrous exercise designed only for show.[19] Participant and spectator blurred into one another in court festivals which imposed the wearing of certain colours on those present. The exaggerated court fashions of the time, with their emphasis on brilliant colour and striking contrast, contributed to the pervasive sense of spectacle and self-display.[20] As I have mentioned, d'Aubigné was no stranger to the court spectacular. If only in passing, he does mention in *Sa Vie* his role in devising court entertainments, including cavalcades, masquerades and ballets. He alludes in particular to a *Circé* which he wrote for Catherine de Médicis for the reception of the Polish ambassadors in 1573, but which she refused to stage for financial reasons.[21]

D'Aubigné's writing censures the inauthenticity of the courtier's existence by privileging essence over appearance. In fact, though, much of his œuvre is in fact deeply imbued with the very theatricality it denounces. *Les Tragiques*, for instance, derives considerable poetic force from its blend of a number of different literary genres — epic, satire, but, most importantly, tragedy. Scholars have used contemporary theoretical writings on tragedy, such as Jean de la Taille's *L'Art de la tragédie* (1572) to illuminate important aspects of *Les Tragiques*, and critics have also detected traces of the influence of mystery plays and Protestant theatre in the poem.[22] The metaphor of the 'world-as-theatre', a Renaissance commonplace, recurs throughout d'Aubigné's writings. The poet's invocation of Melpomene, the muse of tragic poetry, near the beginning of 'Misères' in *Les Tragiques* illustrates this:

> Ici le sang n'est feint, le meurtre n'y defaut,
> La mort jouë elle mesme en ce triste eschaffaut
> Le Juge criminel tourne et emplit son urne.
> D'ici la botte en jambe et non pas le cothurne,
> J'appelle Melpomene en sa vive fureur [...] [23]

Theatricality features in d'Aubigné's prose writing as well. His *Histoire universelle* contains many theatrical effects designed to bring out, from a Protestant perspective, the illusory character of human experience and the value of divine grace and providence.[24] In addition to tragedy, d'Aubigné's writings also betray the influence of comic theatre and the burlesque.[25] For instance, *Les Avantures du Baron de Fæneste*, exposes King Henri IV, an inveterate seducer, as a figure of fun. In a short comic scene, one of the dialogue's interlocutors, the sieur de Beaujeu, a royal guardsman, narrates one of the king's misadventures with a mistress, 'la belle Corisande,' Diane d'Andouins, countess of Guiche (1554–1620):

> Le Roy mesme, pour aller à l'amour, accompagné de Frontenac seul, estant tous deux desguisez de cappes de Bearn blanches, alla en poste à Yemant. Ayant passé Artez, trouva la populace du pays, qui avec bastons ferrez poursuivoit des sorciers; toutes les cloches sonnerent sur lui, et deux cents populaces, qu'à pied, qu'à cheval, les poursuivirent aux rais de la lune, criants, *A la cause, à la cause!* jusques dans le jardin de Yemant, où la Comtesse qui les attendoit, fit le *hola*.[26]

The image of the king, whose disguise of a white cape only makes him all the more conspicuous owing to the comic coincidences of the witch hunt and the full moon, cannot fail to prompt the reader's laughter, and, ultimately, his or her critical reflection on such unregal behaviour.[27]

Like these other works, *Sa Vie* participates in the theatricality characteristic of the general culture of the period and present to a particularly high degree amongst courtiers.[28] At the heart of d'Aubigné's autobiography thus lies an intriguing paradox. *Sa Vie* vehemently rejects the charade and hypocrisy of court life.

However, the means whereby d'Aubigné criticizes the corruption of the court, and simultaneously demonstrates his own exemplary integrity, themselves rely heavily on a kind of courtly play acting — what Gilbert Schrenck has called 'la théatrâlisation et la parade du moi' or 'volonté de mise en scène'.[29] In this respect, *Sa Vie* typifies 'baroque autobiography'. Instead of valorizing interiority, as implied by Lejeune's imperative that autobiography trace 'la genèse d'une personnalité', *Sa Vie* instead shows an entirely baroque sensibility in its exaggerated display of emotion.[30]

D'Aubigné articulated this paradox as early as the dedication of *Sa Vie* to his children, Louise, Constant and Marie. Here, the father apparently rejected any form of theatricality by first asserting that he would present his 'true self' in his autobiography. He would not hide his faults, but instead reveal them to his children 'toutes nues, comme le point qui [...] porte le plus de butin'.[31] This attitude diametrically opposes that prescribed for example by d'Aubigné's contemporary, Francis Bacon (1561–1626) who stressed that the prudent man should possess the acting skill required to 'cover artificially his weaknesses, defects, misfortunes and disgraces'.[32] Second, d'Aubigné claimed that he did not seek a wide audience for his autobiographical performance of his self. On the contrary, in his preface to his children and dedicatees, d'Aubigné insists on the need to limit the circulation of his autobiography. Here, the father strictly enjoins his children not to allow the only two manuscript copies of *Sa Vie* to leave their houses.[33]

Despite this claim to authenticity and rejection of masquerade, d'Aubigné adopts a theatrical persona even at this early point in the text of *Sa Vie*. The rhetoric of the dedicatory preface to his children already suggests an element of role-playing in the autobiography. D'Aubigné imagines *Sa Vie* as a performance aimed at a specific audience. He announces in the preface that he will narrate his triumphs and his flaws to his children 'comme si je vous entretenois encores sur mes genoux'.[34] The rhetorical framework of *Sa Vie* thus images an intimate exchange between the storyteller–protagonist and rapt audience. D'Aubigné plays the role of the wise and benevolent father spinning a fireside tale to amuse his young children. To hold their attention, the narrator may well have recourse to theatrical devices, such as clowning, magic, violence, and use of suspense, all of which we find in the text of *Sa Vie*.[35]

Presented as a family document, and thus at a remove from the corruption of the court, *Sa Vie* nonetheless bears the traces of d'Aubigné's experience of life in the entourage of Henri IV. According to its preface, *Sa Vie* purports to show d'Aubigné's children what they will require to deal with persecution from hostile princes at court: the intellectual qualities of 'dexterité' and 'adresse' which, rather than sheer strength, will enable them to 'porter les fardeaux de dessus'.[36] As d'Aubigné relates, Henri IV disapproved of his favourites reading biographies of the Roman emperors and reproached Bertrand de Melet de Fayolles, seigneur de Neuvy (d. 1589), for excessive attachment to his Tacitus.[37] The king feared that Neuvy would be inspired to imitate the great men depicted by the Roman historian and consequently challenge royal authority. Henri IV wished Neuvy would instead seek out 'quelque vie d'un sien compagnon', that is to say, the biography of someone closer in rank to himself. By including this anecdote in the preface to *Sa Vie*, d'Aubigné presents his autobiography as just such a text: the life of a courtier written for the edification of his fellow courtiers — in this case, his children — with the authorization of the king.[38]

D'Aubigné intimates that his children must acquire the intellectual qualities of 'dexterité' and 'adresse' to survive in an oppressive regime. I would argue that d'Aubigné modelled these qualities in his autobiography by demonstrating his possession of the courtly skills of play-acting and stage-managing. Like d'Aubigné, Montaigne also recognizes the importance of these skills for the courtier when, at the end of 'De l'institution des enfans', he champions the value and usefulness of theatrical performance to the formation of a young nobleman. Not only does Montaigne boast of his own youthful aptitude for play-acting, he points out that he shared this experience of theatrical performance with princes:

> Mettray-je en compte cette faculté de mon enfance: une asseurance de visage, et soupplesse de voix et de geste, à m'appliquer aux rolles que j'entreprenois? Car, avant l'aage, [...] j'ai soustenu les premiers personnages és tragedies latines de Bucanan, de Guerente et de Muret, qui se representerent en nostre college de Guienne avec dignité [...] et m'en tenoit-on maistre ouvrier. C'est un exercice que je ne mesloüe poinct aux jeunes enfans de maison; et ay veu nos Princes s'y adonner depuis en personne, à l'exemple d'aucuns des anciens, honnestement et louablement.[39]

The quality of 'soupplesse' Montaigne observes in himself relates closely to the 'dexterité' and 'adresse' d'Aubigné recommends to his children. Like Bacon's prudent man who can 'set forth to advantage before others, with grace and skill, his virtues, fortunes and merits' and conceal artificially his faults, d'Aubigné hints that he owed his success, or indeed his very survival, to his dexterity, his cunning ability to manipulate appearances. D'Aubigné may well claim that his faults are the most spiritually instructive portion of his autobiography. In fact, the dedication of *Sa Vie* suggests that d'Aubigné's example contains another, more pragmatic lesson: the utility of the noble art of play-acting.

The circumstances of d'Aubigné's early life, as he relates them in *Sa Vie*, unquestionably have a tragic shadow over them. D'Aubigné begins by telling of the untimely death of his mother in giving birth to him. When, six years later, his mother makes a ghostly visitation to him, the scene recalls much of Renaissance tragedy in its fascination with ghosts. Following on from this woeful start in life, his father banished him from the house because of his stepmother's unwillingness to spend much money on his upbringing. Indeed, in terms of its contents, d'Aubigné's autobiography fulfils remarkably closely Jean de la Taille's definition of the true subject of tragedy in *L'Art de la tragédie*:

> Son vray subject ne traicte que de piteuses ruines des grandes seigneurs, que des inconstances de Fortune, que bannissements, guerres, pestes, famines, captivitez, execrables cruautez des Tyrans [...] [40]

But the influence of theatre on d'Aubigné's autobiography transcends the level of the tragic nature of the events recounted. Rather, we find it in a number of recurrent theatrical motifs which endow d'Aubigné's autobiography with a sense of overall unity. In what follows, I shall discuss four main aspects of the theatrical in d'Aubigné's autobiography: costume, use of stage business or props, gesture, and, finally, the presence of an audience.

Costume

In several key scenes in d'Aubigné's autobiography, clothing plays a crucial role in creating a sense of drama and character, and in drawing attention to the author as the main actor. 'Clothing' thus becomes 'costume,' which in French contains an intriguing ambiguity as it can signify at once how one dresses, and one's moral character or habits.[41] Before examining in detail the motif of clothing in *Sa Vie*, it is worth recalling briefly the importance of dress in the creation of the early modern spectacle and, more broadly, as part of the theatre of court life.

Treatises on stagecraft which gave advice to directors of plays, such as the *Quattro dialoghi in materia di rappresentazione sceniche* by Leone de' Sommi (*c.*1525–92), stressed the primordial importance of theatrical dress in attracting and maintaining the spectator's interest.[42] The surviving evidence for sixteenth-century theatrical dress includes a few designs for costumes, written eyewitness accounts of productions and representations of performances on tapestries and paintings.[43] Of particular note is Jacques Thibout's detailed account of the extraordinarily rich costumes worn in Bourges in 1536 in a religious drama, the 'Mysteres des SS Actes des Apostres'.[44] Like many such testimonials, Thibout's account insists on the visually striking costumes. Productions of religious dramas officially ceased in Paris in 1548, owing to the increasing tensions between Catholics and Protestants. However, religious processions continued to take place in great number. Surviving accounts of these attest to their highly theatrical flavour and, specifically, to the elaborate dress worn.[45] Italian theatre companies frequently visited the French court and, as mentioned above, Catherine de Médicis was a generous patron of ballets and masquerades in the Italian taste. Performances of such 'balets de cour' and masquerades generally included splendid theatrical costume, as the lavish illustrations in Robert Boissard's *Mascarades receuillies* (1597) abundantly show.

As for court fashions, their extravagant colours and rich ornamentation often made them difficult to distinguish from theatrical dress. Opulence in clothing affirmed rank. The ability to modify one's sartorial style in line with constantly changing fashions served as a barometer for a courtier's position in the social hierarchy. The baroque court had a taste for brilliant colours and eye-catching contrasts; and only social inferiors uniformly wore the same severe, dark colours.[46]

Throughout d'Aubigné's œuvre, he responded to the baroque culture of appearances by often referring to clothing, both as metaphor and as the object of satire. In the *Tragiques*, for instance, he developed extensively the image of rich clothing used to hide the inner depravity of the court.[47] Similarly, in the *Avantures du Baron de Fæneste*, Enay ridicules the current fashions at court. Enay contends that courtiers spend far too much money on superfluities in dress — for example a fine white lace collar or hose in every conceivable colour — when they lack the resources to cover the essentials (such as a clean undershirt). What is worse, Enay observes, contemporary fashions themselves are impractical and may even have a deleterious effect on health:

> Enay. Comment paroist-on aujourdh'hui à la Cour? — Fæneste. Premierement faut estre vien vestu à la mode de trois ou quatre Messurs qui ont l'autorité: il faut un perpunt de quatre ou cinq taffetas l'un sur l'autre, des chausses comme celles que bous boyez, dans lesquelles, tant frise qu'escarlatte, je bous puis assurer de huict aulnes d'estoffe pour le mens. — E. Est-il possible que ce gros lodier qui vous monte autour des reins ne vous fasse point sentir la gravelle?[48]

The expense of court dress made it a favoured means of bribery.[49] D'Aubigné repudiates this specific form of corruption in the 'Elégie autobiographique':

> J'ay porté du village à la cour mes humeurs:
> Je voulus estre en court plus amy qu'acostable
> Et pour monstre nouveau courtizan veritable,
> Embrasser de mon Maistre et la vie et l'ennuy,
> L'honneur et le secret et les maux plus que luy,
> N'avoir jamais de luy or, *vestement*, ne terre [...][50]

If d'Aubigné satirized the contemporary fixation with luxurious fashions elsewhere in his œuvre, in *Sa Vie* he retained a baroque awareness of dress as a means of creating spectacle. Early modern biographers do on occasion attend to their subjects' dress, but in a far more perfunctory manner than d'Aubigné. For example, Nancel remarked upon Ramus's clothing in order to point out its modest austerity and thereby underline the philosopher's sober moral character.[51] Nancel's comments follow the Erasmian dictum that garments should accord with inner character. As Erasmus wrote in *De civilitate morum puerilium* (1530, Fr. trans. 1537): 'clothing is in a way the body's body, and from this too one may infer the state of a man's character'. D'Aubigné's autobiography engages creatively with the humanistic notion that outer garments can and should display inner character, making it a highly productive source of theatrical effect.[52] What is more, references to clothing in *Sa Vie* tend to come at particularly dramatic points in the text, where d'Aubigné's social identity is at stake. D'Aubigné's concern to advertise his status as a *gentilhomme* in *Sa Vie* tallies with George Huppert's depiction of him as an adventurer of dubious nobility who sought to consolidate his material fortune and thus his social position through marriage to a wealthy heiress — a strategy he was to repeat as an elderly widower, when his fortune was in need of restoration.[53] The precise circumstances of this first marriage do not feature in *Sa Vie*: the marriage contract of June 1583 cites d'Aubigné as owner of a substantial seigneurie, a property which he had 'acquired' only days before, on the security of payment after his marriage.

D'Aubigné's volubility in vestimentary matters in *Sa Vie* contrasts with the reticence he expresses in the preface to the *Histoire universelle* about representation of his physical appearance:

> Les Imprimeurs sont curieux de representer en taille douce les Autheurs aux premieres pages de leurs livres: tel soin est inutile, car il ne profite point au Lecteur, de voir le visage et les lineamens de celui qui l'enseigne; mais bien ceux de l'ame, pour recevoir les jugemens des choses avec le trebuchet en main.[54]

Here, d'Aubigné categorically rejects author portraits because they cannot reveal inner, spiritual truth. In *Sa Vie*, however, the repeated references to clothing as a device for indicating character suggest a different attitude to appearances, and certainly, d'Aubigné also seems better disposed to pictorial representation of appearances. Near the beginning of his autobiography, d'Aubigné relates how he translated Plato's *Crito* at the tender age of seven, 'avec quelque aide de ses leçons'.[55] He undertook this difficult task: 'sur la promesse du père qu'il le feroit imprimer avec l'effigie enfantine au devant du livre'. But d'Aubigné relegates to his childhood this desire to have an image of himself made and published. His unwillingness to comment in his autobiography on his corporeal person betrays a Calvinist scruple about focus on the self, which could only constitute an obstacle to knowledge of the divine.[56] And it is true that in *Sa Vie* d'Aubigné never provides even a cursory description of his bodily aspect, such as those found in Nancel's *Life of Ramus* or Binet's *Vie de Ronsard*.[57]

Still, d'Aubigné does not extend this silence about his body to all aspects of his material existence. In *Sa Vie*, he is finely attuned to the value of dress, not only in terms of its ability to create spectacle and to focus attention but also to signal noble identity. As I have already mentioned, dress in the early modern period was an important signifier of social identity. Each professional or social group had its own distinctive apparel and accoutrements, such as nobles with their swords and short capes, magistrates in their long gowns and bonnets (*gens de robe longue*), friars and monks in the robes of their orders and prostitutes with ear rings.[58] Furthermore, sumptuary laws — there were 18 edicts published in France from 1485 to 1660 — represented an attempt, however futile, to regulate dress precisely according to socio-economic class.[59]

The existence of such sumptuary codes made it possible for d'Aubigné to use clothing to lay claim to a noble identity right from the outset of *Sa Vie*. The first mention of dress occurs when he is ten years old. In around 1562, together with his teacher Mathieu Béroalde (1516–76) and a small group of fellow Protestants, d'Aubigné fled religious persecution in Paris. Travelling through Courance, south of Paris, the party fell into the hands of the Catholic Chevalier d'Achon and his men, who conveyed them to an inquisitor. D'Aubigné underlines his boyish bravery by relating that, despite the evident danger, he did not initially show any outward signs of fear. He broke down only when his captors divested him of a child-sized silver sword and the silver belt on which he wore it. His attachment to this precious item of clothing shows a significant degree of self-conscious pride. Even at this tender age, d'Aubigné's concern for the small sword reveals him to be thoroughly cognizant of his future role as a soldier for his faith. Because of the luxurious material of his costume, D'Achon's men took him aside for separate interrogation: 'les Capitaines qui luy voyoient un habillement de satin blanc, bandé de broderie d'argent, et quelque façon qui leur plaisoit, l'amenerent en la chambre d'Achon'.[60] D'Aubigné carefully furnishes these details of his clothing and gesture ('quelque façon qui leur plaisoit') in order to portray his boyish self as being already the principal actor in the narration of his life. That d'Achon's men singled him out is in keeping with another motif which runs throughout the text of his autobiography:

that of d'Aubigné as belonging to the religious elect. D'Aubigné pauses over the details of his costume here in order for the reader of his autobiography to be able to visualize the scene as vividly as possible and thus to identify with its youthful protagonist. In this short scene, depiction of costume forms the prelude to the performance of dramatic dialogue, as there follows a spirited exchange between d'Aubigné and his Catholic tormentors.[61] When the captors tempt him to abjure by threatening to burn all the prisoners at the stake, d'Aubigné retorts that his horror of the mass far outweighs that of the martyr's pyre.

Possession of aristocratic apparel — white satin and silver brocade — is the motor behind the dramatic clash with his Catholic captors from which d'Aubigné emerges triumphant: he has performed as a true nobleman and a faithful Protestant. D'Aubigné further asserts his noble identity and his entitlement to gentleman's clothes in an equally theatrical, if rather more comic than potentially tragic, confrontation with his father, Jean. Also a military man, Jean d'Aubigné made an impromptu visit to his son during a journey through Guyenne. He found his son in good health (having recently recovered from a bout of plague), but he worried that the boy had become debauched and was neglecting his literary studies: 'comme il est difficile *Pacis artes colere, inter Martis incendia*', as Agrippa remarked, reinforcing the message with a Latin tag.[62] This prompted the father to send his son 'un habillement de Bureau' — a thick and coarse cloth, of brown russet, or some dark colour — and bid him to seek out an occupation in some lowly trade, since he had abandoned 'les lettres et l'honneur'. Needless to say, this paternal reproach devastated d'Aubigné. After becoming seriously ill again in reaction, the boy once more redeemed himself by his acting skills. He demonstrated his capacity to move an audience to pity when he fell to his knees before his father and pronounced a lengthy harangue which brought tears to his listeners' eyes. Just as there could be no question of his wearing anything other than the finest fabrics, so there could be no doubt of d'Aubigné's nobility.

Once he has established his noble identity, d'Aubigné seems to become less attached to clothing. Indeed, he signals his coming of age and simultaneous transformation into a Protestant soldier by leaving behind his clothes.[63] In 1568, the sixteen-year-old d'Aubigné, now an orphan, yearns to test his mettle on the battlefield in the service of his faith. His guardians attempt to prevent him from escaping to fight by confiscating his clothing every night. This fails to stop the determined would-be soldier. D'Aubigné ties his sheets into a rope to climb out through his bedroom window barefoot and in his white nightshirt. He rejoins his comrades in arms, who are surprised to see him running after them and calling out, crying because his feet were bleeding. Here too, attention to detail of costume (or lack of it) makes the scene theatrical and adds to the impression of d'Aubigné's heroism. As in the previous two episodes, the response of the internal audience of the autobiography models that of the reader: the spectators to d'Aubigné's actions admire the dramatic feats carried out by the hero. The band's leader, the Capitaine Sainct Lo, gives him a cloak, in order to spare his tender bottom from being scraped raw by the buckle on the horse's saddle. A short while later, d'Aubigné refuses to rob the band's Catholic victims of their clothing. He prefers instead to wait until they arrive at the nearest town in order legitimately to acquire something to wear. This echoes the pattern set in the earlier confrontation with d'Achon's men: dress triggers a mini-drama which d'Aubigné concludes with a witty moralizing retort. This time, he delivers his riposte in written form rather than as a verbal 'response'. D'Aubigné quotes the inscription he appended to the bill of sale for his new set of clothing: 'Il mit au bout de sa sedulle, *A la charge que je ne reprocheroys point à la guerre qu'elle m'a despouillé, n'en pouvant sortir plus mal equippé que je n'y entre*.'[64]

A number of similar episodes later in *Sa Vie* likewise emphasize d'Aubigné's bravery as a soldier by focusing on his lack of protective garments.[65] During the siege of Marmande in 1577, d'Aubigné displays his bravery and his soldierly prowess by ceremoniously removing his arm-plate as nobody else has one. He also fights with his sword in his left hand to protect a lock of his mistress's hair.[66] D'Aubigné figures as a heroic knight, who fights for personal honour and his mistress's favour, in total disregard for the perils of combat. By his dramatic unconcern for dress, he paradoxically creates a spectacle every bit as striking as if he were to parade in the most extravagant raiment, like the appearance-obsessed soldiers in the *Avantures du Baron de Fæneste* who conspicuously ride into battle astride plumed horses and insist on wearing scarlet doublets covered with silver embroidery. This scene serves to reinsert *Sa Vie* within the courtly context. D'Aubigné's knightly behaviour here recalls the chivalric courtesy of the tournament rather than the brutal mayhem of civil war. The element of courtly spectacle in this scene palliates the reader's sense of actual danger. Indeed, two years earlier whilst at the Valois court, d'Aubigné had performed in just such a tournament before his beloved Diane Salviati.[67]

The motif of costume in d'Aubigné's autobiography thus performs a dual function. Strikingly present, it establishes his noble identity; dramatically absent, it signifies the hero's moral superiority to those with power over him within the court context.[68]

Stage Business

In addition to costume, what might be termed props or stage business represent another important way in which d'Aubigné creates courtly spectacle in his autobiography. This features prominently in two scenes which occur close together in the text, and which function along similar narrative lines. In both of these episodes, d'Aubigné uses his talents not only as a poet, but even more crucially, as 'metteur en scène' to direct events and criticize his master, Henri de Navarre. The unusual means by which d'Aubigné communicates his discontent with Henri attenuates the harshness of his criticism. D'Aubigné cunningly uses entertainment, or surprise, to render more palatable his dissenting views. At the same time, though, the dramatic nature of these scenes effectively guarantees that d'Aubigné gets his point across.

The first occurs in 1577 when d'Aubigné is passing through Agen after the peace of Bergerac, which had put an end to the sixth of the wars of religion.[69] He has just quoted his letter of resignation from the service of Henri de Navarre, owing to his disgust at Henri's corrupt ways, and, in particular, his carelessness of faithful servants. This letter, a highly declamatory composition, tells how d'Aubigné's twelve years in the prince's service correspond to twelve wounds on his stomach. D'Aubigné reminds his former master that the hand which is writing the letter is the same one which was responsible for unlocking the bars of Navarre's prison.[70] Still, the scene which follows shows a theatricality which surpasses the epistolary rhetoric. In Agen, d'Aubigné stays with Madame de Roques, who had been a source of support for him in times of trouble. Here, d'Aubigné comes upon a spaniel named Citron, whom he recognizes as the dog which used to sleep at the prince's feet, between d'Aubigné himself and another friend, Frontenac. This dog, a former intimate of Navarre, has himself now fallen on hard times, and d'Aubigné says that he is starving. Nonetheless, Citron greets d'Aubigné with a warm display of canine affection. Moved by this, d'Aubigné sees to the dog's care, arranging for him to stay with a local lady. The discovery of Citron inspires him to write a sonnet criticizing the prince's ingratitude and forgetfulness of former faithful servants, which he then sews into the dog's collar. When Henri later arrives in Agen, the dog, with its embroidered collar, is shown to him as a curiosity. Upon reading the sonnet, with its critical message, Navarre is upset and, as d'Aubigné points out, changes colour. D'Aubigné uses the dog Citron to stage his disgruntlement as a courtier at being neglected by his master.

Some years after this daring 'coup de théâtre', d'Aubigné creates a similar tableau for Navarre which he receives with slightly better grace, probably owing to an improvement in their relationship at this moment. Passing through Cadillac, Navarre asks the scholar and mathematician François de Foix, comte de Candale (1502–94), to show him his famous cabinet of curiosities.[71] Candale agrees, provided that only those capable of appreciating his collection with due seriousness be admitted to view it. Navarre assures Candale that he will be accompanied only by a select group of worthy individuals, including d'Aubigné. While the rest of the group marvels at a special mechanical device that allows a six-year old child to lift a heavy cannon, d'Aubigné slips away unnoticed. He goes on ahead, stopping at an impressive, seven-foot square piece of black marble in which Candale kept his notebooks behind a curtain. As Navarre and his companions chat about the weight-lifting machine, d'Aubigné goes in search of a brush and ink, and proceeds quickly to scrawl a Latin distich in one of Candale's notebooks. The bold Latin poem admonishes Navarre that princes ought not to play with toy weights, but rather learn to bear the burden of power with a deft hand. D'Aubigné then covers over his artwork with the curtain and awaits the arrival of the rest of the group. When the others appear, Candale draws back the curtain to reveal his notebooks, takes one out and finds d'Aubigné's poem. He responds, in recognition of the audacity of d'Aubigné's poetic comment, by exclaiming: 'O il y a ici un homme!' Navarre retorts to his uncle: 'Tenez vous le reste pour des bestes?'[72] Navarre's response indicates his pleasure that his entourage be characterized as one where liberty and frank speech among nobles prevails. D'Aubigné's use of the theatrical device of the curtain and the poem hidden in the book, which provides an added element of surprise, suggests a role for him as the one who reveals the truth concealed behind surface appearances. He communicates this by means of the written word, and in Latin, in keeping with his identity as an intellectual and a man of letters. D'Aubigné's poetic composition prompts the exchange between Candale and Navarre, who enact his political message by confirming that princes must uphold the freedom of their noble courtiers. Directing the theatre as always, d'Aubigné has constructed an entire stage set out of Candale's private museum, together with props and secondary actors. He adroitly mobilizes all of this material to guarantee the maximum emotional response from the internal audience — those present at Candale's museum — as well as, ultimately, from the reader of the autobiography.

Gesture

D'Aubigné performs a similar role as 'metteur en scène' at numerous other points in *Sa Vie*. Many of these depend on d'Aubigné instructing his fellow courtiers to perform a certain gesture in order to achieve a particular effect. Such gesture, often of paramount importance in the autobiography, typically reinforces a rhetorical point in much the same way as the visual details of costume, or the use of props. For instance, one of Navarre's men, François de Ségur, appears to waver in his loyalty to the Protestant cause, and D'Aubigné discovers that Ségur sympathizes with a Catholic faction that wanted Navarre go to the French court, where his conversion to Catholicism was likely.[73] D'Aubigné responds to Ségur's betrayal by first leading him to a window in the Chateau de Nérac which overlooked the gorge of a river; he then threatens Ségur with defenestration, should Navarre leave his kingdom for the French court. Ségur, shocked, asks who would dare to carry out such an act. D'Aubigné replies that if he cannot do it alone, he has supporters to help him and points at ten strong men who immediately pull their hats down over their heads. D'Aubigné had ordered them to perform this gesture before he approached Ségur, but without telling the men exactly what he was plotting. The reader thus has the impression of a skilled courtier in control of any situation, able to manipulate those around him and make them fulfil his every command.

Audience

The presence of an internal audience to witness and admire d'Aubigné's actions constitutes the final element of theatre found in *Sa Vie*. Bouwsma has written about early modern theatre's capacity, in a society fragmented by social change, to unite people. Through the shared experience of the play, theatre created a small, if temporary, community.[74] D'Aubigné certainly makes use of theatre's power to assemble and unite an audience, rallying it to his cause.[75] Although d'Aubigné himself indisputably has the main billing as the principal actor in his autobiography, he devotes careful attention to the way in which others respond to his actions. D'Aubigné thus makes his reader constantly aware of his life as being a bravura performance which takes place before an audience. D'Aubigné reveals himself to be a keen observer of the expressions and countenances of others, invariably supplying information about the expression on the faces of his spectators and their attitude to his actions, which is generally one of admiration. For example, he tells how he put this ability to work for him when called upon to protect the Château de Montaigu, a Huguenot stronghold, in 1580. In one year, the Catholics attempted ten attacks against the fortress, but D'Aubigné successfully foiled these attacks, thanks to his skill in physiognomy, the science of face-reading.

I have mentioned how the rhetorical preface to *Sa Vie* highlights the importance of audience by comparing the written text to a tale told to his children as if he still held them on his knees. Audience remains central throughout the text of the autobiography. For instance, in the early inquisition scene with d'Achon and his men, a dance — bizarre as this may seem — follows the interrogation. The soldiers ask d'Aubigné to perform a 'gaillarde', and the child accepts the invitation to dance for d'Achon's men, thus providing yet more evidence of courage in the face of so many armed enemies. His willingness to comply, combined, one presumes, with his talent for dance, fills the assembled audience with admiration and even love for the boy. A short time later, d'Aubigné takes refuge at the court of Renée de France, duchess of Ferrara (1510–75). The duchess has the child sit on a cushion near her in order that she may hear him speak on the contempt for death.[76] As a soldier in the third round of religious wars (1570), he falls gravely ill with fever, and his agony and speeches of contrition for his wrongdoings during previous battles makes the hairs stand up on the heads of those who visit his sickbed.[77]

D'Aubigné's emphasis on audience response in *Sa Vie* intriguingly echoes contemporary developments in theoretical writings on tragedy. For example, Jean de la Taille argued in his *De l'art de la tragédie* for the dependence of tragedy on representation. According to La Taille, the public was as necessary to the creation of tragedy as the play and its actors.[78] Through the use of the motif of clothing and costume, so central to the Renaissance stage,[79] as well as a preoccupation with stagecraft and dramatic gesture, d'Aubigné creates an autobiography with a thoroughly theatrical flavour. D'Aubigné's narrative of his life to his children does not provide the introspective account of the genesis of personality which, after Petrarch or Montaigne, we have come to expect of the autobiographical mode of writing. Rather, in *Sa Vie à ses enfants*, d'Aubigné puts on a spectacular performance of self designed for consumption by an audience. Although d'Aubigné's autobiography certainly does narrate his Protestant religious vocation, it is more than a 'récit parabolique' designed for moral instruction and individual meditation. Rather, d'Aubigné sought to teach his children how to withstand persecution from hostile princes at court by presenting them with his own example. This paternal model consisted in large measure of the courtly survival skills of play-acting and stage-management. D'Aubigné's use of the discourse of theatricality in his autobiographical construction of self aligns *Sa Vie* with the four examples of biography discussed in the previous chapters. Each of these texts similarly exploits a particular discourse to fashion a certain kind of subject: philosophy and history for Le Roy's Budé; the art of diplomacy with Paschal's Pibrac; the mercurial figure of the courtier-poet for Binet's Ronsard; and medicine in the case of Nancel's Ramus. Although, as an autobiography, *Sa Vie* may not quite fit the model of a text written about another in the interest of one's own social and career advancement, it certainly shares with these other works a central preoccupation with self-legitimation.

Notes to Chapter 5

1. On the date of composition of *Sa Vie*, see Gilbert Schrenck, 'Introduction', in Agrippa d'Aubigné, *Sa Vie à ses enfants*, ed. by Gilbert Schrenck (Paris: Nizet, 1986), pp. 11–36 (pp. 16–17). Further references to the text of *Sa Vie* are to this edition.
2. Schrenck, 'Introduction', p. 27.
3. *GBV*, pp. 17–20. Schrenck, 'Aspects de l'écriture autobiographique au XVIe siècle: A. d'Aubigné et *Sa Vie à ses Enfants*', *Nouvelle Revue du Seizième Siècle*, 3 (1985), 31–51 (pp. 46–47).
4. *Sa Vie*, pp. 85–91. Schrenck, 'Aspects', p. 45.
5. Schrenck, 'Introduction', pp. 30–32.
6. Nadine Kuperty-Tsur, 'Aspects de la rhétorique d'Agrippa d'Aubigné dans *Sa Vie à ses enfants*', *Albineana*, 13 (2001), 105–18 (p. 111 and p. 117).
7. Frances A. Yates, *The Valois Tapestries*, 2nd edn (London: Routledge & Kegan Paul, 1975), pp. 51–55 and p. 105. Jacqueline Boucher, *La Cour de Henri III* (Rennes: Ouest-France, 1986), pp. 123–25.
8. Schrenck, 'Aspects', p. 40. Philippe Lejeune, *L'Autobiographie en France* (Paris: A. Colin, 1971), p. 85.
9. Kuperty-Tsur, 'Aspects de la rhétorique', p. 110.
10. William Bouwsma, *The Waning of the Renaissance, 1550–1640* (New Haven, CT: Yale University Press, 2000), p. 131.
11. 'Princes' in *Les Tragiques*, ed. by Jean-Raymond Fanlo, 2 vols (Paris: Honoré Champion, 1995), I, 2, vv. 1175–1485. All subsequent references to the *Tragiques* are to this edition. I. D. McFarlane, 'Introduction', in Agrippa d'Aubigné, *Les Tragiques*, ed. by I. D. McFarlane (London: Athlone Press, 1970), p. 5.
12. 'Princes', vv. 1259–66.
13. 'Princes', vv. 1281–84.
14. D'Aubigné, *Œuvres complètes*, ed. by Henri Weber, Jacques Bailbé and Marguerite Soulié (Paris: Gallimard, 1969), p. 671 and p. 1347.
15. *Les Avantures du Baron de Fæneste*, in d'Aubigné, *Œuvres complètes*, p. 679.
16. For the circumstances of composition of the 'Elégie autobiographique', see d'Aubigné, *Œuvres complètes*, p. 326, note 1.
17. Boucher, 'La Cour', pp. 123–24.
18. Ibid., p. 123.
19. Yates, 'Valois Tapestries', pp. 51–53 and p. 105.
20. Boucher, 'La Cour', pp. 72–73. Daniel Roche, *La Culture des apparances. Une histoire du vêtement. XVIIe — XVIIIe siècle* (Paris: Fayard, 1989), p. 45.
21. *Sa Vie*, p. 85. On the fortune of this work, see *Sa Vie*, p. 85, note 121. Henri III would later put on a festival treating the *Circé* myth choreographed by Balthazar de Beaujoyeulx for the 1581 wedding of his favourite, the Duc de Joyeuse. Margaret McGowan dismisses d'Aubigné's claim that Beaujoyeulx stole this *Circé* from him. See *Le Balet comique by Balthazar de Beaujoyeulx, 1581*, a facsimile with an introduction by Margaret M. McGowan (Binghampton, NY: Centre for Medieval and Renaissance Studies, 1982), p. 37.
22. Jacques Bailbé, *Agrippa d'Aubigné, poète des Tragiques* (Caen: Association des publications de la faculté des Lettres et Sciences humaines, 1968); Richard Regosin, 'D'Aubigné's *Les Tragiques*: Divine Tragedy', *Bibliothèque d'Humanisme et Renaissance*, 28 (1966), 52–73.
23. 'Misères,' vv. 75–79. See also 'Princes' vv. 206–14 and 'Les Feux' vv. 819–24. On the 'world-as-theatre' metaphor, see Bouwsma, 'Waning', p. 132.
24. Mitchell Greenberg, 'Baroque History: Style and Structure in the "Histoire Universelle"' (unpublished doctoral dissertation, University of California at Berkeley, 1973; abstract in *Dissertation abstracts*, 27.9, 5815-A).
25. Christian Fantoni , 'Henri IV burlesque dans *Les avantures du Baron de Fæneste* d'Agrippa d'Aubigné', *Nouvelle revue du XVIe siècle*, 19.2 (2001), 69–81.
26. *Les Avantures du Baron de Fæneste*, in d'Aubigné, *Œuvres complètes*, p. 786.
27. Ibid..
28. Bouwsma, 'Waning', pp. 131–42.

29. Schrenck, 'Aspects', p. 50; Schrenck 'A. d'Aubigné, *Sa Vie à ses Enfants*. Approches et mises en perspective', *Réforme Humanisme Renaissance*, 10 (1979), 3–11 (pp. 7–8). See also Jean Plattard, *Agrippa d'Aubigné. Une figure de premier plan dans nos Lettres de la Renaissance* (Paris: Boivin, 1931), p. 13 and Kuperty-Tsur, 'Aspects de la rhétorique', p. 110.
30. Philippe Lejeune, *Le Pacte autobiographique* (Paris: Seuil, 1975), p. 14. On the baroque penchant for external display of emotion, see Boucher, 'La Cour', pp. 124–25.
31. *Sa Vie*, p. 49.
32. Cited in Bouwsma, 'Waning', p. 134.
33. *Sa Vie*, 49. Catherine Randall Coats argues that d'Aubigné must have sought a readership beyond that explicitly designated, since his children would not have required his extensive descriptions of familiar facts. Randall Coats, 'Representing and Re-Presenting the Self: Fact and Fiction in Agrippa d'Aubigné's "Sa Vie à Ses Enfants" and the "Histoire Universelle"', *South Atlantic Review*, 54.2 (May 1989), 23–40 (p. 36).
34. *Sa Vie*, p. 49.
35. Bouwsma discusses these as the principal elements constituting the pleasure of the theatre in the early modern period ('Waning', p. 131).
36. *Sa Vie*, p. 48.
37. *Sa Vie*, p. 48.
38. Many nobles at the court of Henri III compiled such instruction manuals for court life for their sons. For examples, see Boucher, 'La Cour', pp. 53–54.
39. *Essais*, I. 26, p. 176.
40. Jean de la Taille, *L'Art de la tragédie*, ed. by Frederick West (Manchester: Manchester University Press, 1939), p. 24.
41. Roche, 'Apparances', p. 12. Compare the polysemous English 'habit'.
42. See in particular 'Dialogo terzo', in Leone de' Sommi, *Quattro dialoghi in materia di rappresentazione sceniche*, ed. by Ferruccio Marotti (Milan: Edizioni Il Polifilo, 1968), pp. 48–53. Written in the early 1570s, this work remained unpublished until the twentieth century.
43. Stella Mary Newton, *Renaissance Theatre Costume and the Sense of the Historic Past* (London: Rapp & Whiting, 1975), pp. 222–66. Yates, 'Valois Tapestries', pp. 13–14.
44. Newton, 'Renaissance Theatre Costume', pp. 222–32. This play was performed again in Paris in 1541.
45. Boucher relates a spectacular torchlight epiphany procession through the Parisian quartier de Saint Antoine organized by the cardinal de Birague ('La Cour', pp. 123–24).
46. Boucher, 'La Cour', pp. 72–74. Roche, 'Apparances', p. 18 and p. 45.
47. James P. Gilroy 'The Theme of "Etre" and "Paraître" in the Works of Agrippa d'Aubigné', *The Bulletin of the Rocky Mountain Modern Language Association*, 27 (1973), 205–11 (p. 206 and p. 209). See especially 'Princes' (vv. 850–900) and the allegorical depiction of Ambition in 'La Chambre dorée' (vv. 265–73).
48. *Avantures du Baron de Fæneste*, in d'Aubigné, *Œuvres complètes*, p. 677.
49. Valentin Groebner, 'Inside Out: Clothes, Dissimulation, and the Arts of Accounting in the Autobiography of Matthaus Schwarz, 1496–1574', *Representations*, 66 (1999), 100–21 (pp. 108–09).
50. 'Elégie autobiographique', vv. 142–49. Patrons often remunerated poets who composed works for court spectacles not only in money but also with pieces of costly fabric as an invitation to harmonize their dress with that of the court (Boucher, 'La Cour', p. 72).
51. *Vita Rami*, p. 238.
52. At least one, admittedly idiosyncratic, Renaissance autobiography did attempt to relate the story of a life entirely through clothing: the manuscript 'Book of Clothes' (*Trachtenbuch*) produced by Matthaus Schwartz (1496–1574), a book-keeper from Augsburg. The *Trachtenbuch* contains 137 portraits of Schwartz by various artists. Accompanied by texts in Schwartz's hand, each portrait gives details of the garments worn and his age, starting from a picture of him as a baby in diapers and finishing with him as an old man, as a mourner at Anton Fugger's funeral in 1560. As Groebner remarks, through the array of clothing illustrated in the *Trachtenbuch*, Schwartz presents himself as a 'scintillating self in series' ('Inside Out', p. 117). Recording changes in clothing thus communicates permutations in the self: self-*fashioning* in the sartorial sense.

53. Huppert, *Les Bourgeois Gentilshommes*, p. 144.
54. *Histoire universelle*, ed. by André Thierry, 11 vols (Geneva: Droz, 1981–2000), I , 9.
55. *Sa Vie*, pp. 51–52.
56. See, however, his reference to stomach wounds sustained in battle (*Sa Vie*, p. 107). On this Calvinist problematic, see Randall Coats, 'Representing and Re-Presenting the Self', pp. 24–25.
57. This may also have to do with the explicitly designated readership of *Sa Vie*: D'Aubigné's children would have known what he looked like.
58. Michael A. Mullet, *The Catholic Reformation* (London: Routledge, 1999), p. 52.
59. Roche, 'Apparances', pp. 44–55.
60. *Sa Vie*, p. 55.
61. This exchange belongs to a set of similar ripostes identified by Ullrich Langer in his article, 'Poétique de la *responce* dans *Sa Vie à ses enfants*', in *Poétiques d'Aubigné*, ed. by Olivier Pot (Geneva: Droz, 1999), pp. 207–16.
62. *Sa Vie*, p. 59.
63. Roche notes the use of 'métamorphoses vestimentaires' in the early novel and their 'fonction de marquage social' ('Apparances', p. 26).
64. *Sa Vie*, p. 66.
65. For instance, in 1586, at the battle of Oléron, d'Aubigné wore only his shirt, except for two occasions on which he donned a helmet (*Sa Vie*, p. 137). Contrast the attitude satirized in the *Avantures du Baron de Fæneste*, in which the elaborate costumes worn by soldiers and their horses serve the needs of 'paroistre', but are woefully unsuited to warfare. The soldiers' excessive love for their beautiful clothes and shiny, spurred boots generally has ridiculous or even disastrous consequences in battle. See *Avantures du Baron de Fæneste*, book 4, chapters 1, 2 and 15.
66. *Sa Vie*, p. 100. Randall Coats, 'Representing and Re-presenting the Self', pp. 35–36.
67. *Sa Vie*, pp. 87–88.
68. For instance, Henri de Navarre destroys d'Aubigné's clothing in a fit of rage at his refusal to act as the prince's pimp. *Sa Vie*, p. 98.
69. *Sa Vie*, p. 107.
70. D'Aubigné alludes here to Navarre's 1576 escape from the Louvre. *Sa Vie*, p. 107, note 204.
71. *Sa Vie*, pp. 121–22.
72. *Sa Vie*, p. 122.
73. *Sa Vie*, p. 129.
74. Bouwsma, 'Waning', p. 133.
75. The martyrology section of 'Les Feux' in *Les Tragiques* displays a similar awareness of the importance of gathering an audience. Here, Montalchine (Giovanni Mollio, martyred at Rome in 1553) moves his audience in a manner unforeseen by his executioners (see 'Les Feux', vv. 639–46).
76. *Sa Vie*, p. 57. Randall Coats discusses this scene as an instance of 'textual exhibitionism' in *Sa Vie*. She argues that d'Aubigné's desire for an audience in his autobiography indicates his aim for a readership beyond that explicitly designated in the preface (his children) ('Representing and Re-presenting the Self', p. 36).
77. *Sa Vie*, p. 74.
78. Jean de la Taille, *De l'art de la tragédie*, pp. 28–29.
79. On the centrality of clothing in Renaissance theatre as well as for self-fashioning on the stage, see 'The circulation of clothes and the making of the English theatre', in Ann Rosalind Jones and Peter Stallybrass, *Renaissance Clothing and the Materials of Memory* (Cambridge: Cambridge University Press, 2000), pp. 175–206.

CONCLUSION

> To write the life of him who excelled all mankind in writing the lives of others, and who, whether we consider his extraordinary endowments, or his various works, has been equalled by few in any age, is an arduous, and may be reckoned in me a presumptuous task.
>
> BOSWELL, *Life of Johnson*, opening sentence

I began this book at the deathbed of the great Guillaume Budé, every detail of whose final illness and agony were piously chronicled in the year of his death by a young Louis Le Roy. By contrast, here is what Le Roy's own nineteenth-century biographer, Abraham Henri Becker, had to say about his subject's eventual demise:

> Le Roy s'était éteint dans l'isolement amer d'une pauvreté orgueilleuse. Nul de songea de faire pour lui ce qu'il avait fait pour d'autres. Ni parmi les lecteurs du roi, ses collègues, ni parmi les savants contemporains, personne ne fixa, dans un latin ému, les traits essentiels d'une existence consacrée aux nobles études. Pour tout oraison funèbre, il eut un sonnet : Antoine de Cotel, conseiller au parlement de Paris et poète à ses heures, déposa sur la tombe de Regius cette couronne funéraire où il y a bien des épines.[1]

Besides the minor poet Antoine de Cotel (1550–1610), amongst Le Roy's contemporaries, Scévole de Sainte-Marthe (1536–1623) devoted one scant page of his collected *Elogia virorum doctrina illustrium* (1598) to the Hellenist, royalist pamphleteer and author of the *Vicissitude*. The erudite historian Jacques-Auguste De Thou (1553–1617) simply repeated Sainte-Marthe's account in the treatment of Le Roy he inserted into his selection of eulogies of learned men of his time. Thereafter, posterity maintained a fairly complete silence surrounding Le Roy's life and works until Becker's 1896 study. With the outrage that betokens a biographer's passion for his subject, Becker lamented that subsequent generations had consistently failed to cite Le Roy amongst those humanists who made significant contributions to Greek studies in France, to the development of the French language or indeed to the history of ideas. 'Est-ce justice?' Becker concluded his own brief summary of Le Roy's existence by posing the rhetorical question.[2]

In the middle of the following century, scholars began to redress the balance somewhat, with Gundersheimer's monograph on Le Roy,[3] and a number of articles and chapters devoted to him in studies of sixteenth-century historiography and translation practices. Still, the giant Budé continues to overshadow his junior colleague and biographer. Much the same applies to the other biographers studied in the preceding chapters, none of whom has been the subject of a book-length study, despite the significance of their contributions to the theory of diplomacy and to political science in the case of Paschal, or to the history of medicine and the development of Ramism in the case of Nancel. Binet, who abandoned the composition of occasional verse relatively early in life to pursue his magisterial career, might arguably be safely relegated to the ranks of minor poets hardly worth a footnote from historians of literature. Still, he contributed importantly to the shaping of Ronsard's future reputation through his work as that poet's literary executor and his *Vie de Ronsard* provides valuable evidence for the contemporary understanding of the relationship between courtiership and poetry.[4]

If these early modern biographers did not make much of an impact on their immediate posterity, they did leave compelling traces of themselves in the biographies they wrote. As I have attempted to show, their manipulation of a particular kind of discourse — theatrical, medical, diplomatic, courtly, philosophical or historical — to represent their biographical subjects significantly inflected the generic canons of epideictic rhetoric central to early modern biography.[5] This transformation of the conventional topics belonging to the rhetoric of praise made the heroes of their biographies exemplary figures who simultaneously broadcast something about the biographer's own social or cultural ambitions. Thus we might best classify such texts generically as hybrids, just as Sisman has described Boswell's *Life of Johnson*: 'a memoir concealed within a life'.[6] A biographer's own life is inevitably imbricated in any account of his biographical subject. My contention has been, furthermore, that the resemblance we may detect between a biographer and his subject, like that of Narcissus gazing into his reflective pool, is hardly a chance affair.

On the contrary, early modern biographers blurred the boundaries between biography and autobiography by exploiting the life narrative of their subjects to prescript their own careers. Biography became not only an act of textual representation of a pre-existing model, but also a projection of the future self of the biographer. In the case of these early modern biographies, exemplarity would thus function at multiple levels, encompassing the biographical subject, the biographer himself, and ultimately, the reader. In selecting his subject, the biographer chose a model he might profitably imitate both textually and extra-textually. This element of emulation suggests a functional utility for early modern biography which complements its rhetorical dimension as a text in praise of a great personage. As I hypothesized in the introduction, a biographer's recreation of his subject in the text both promoted and vouchsafed his unique suitability to follow in the footsteps of his model outside the confines of the text. Such a narrowing of the gap between biography and autobiography has allowed me to include d'Aubigné's *Sa Vie à ses enfants* within this study as a text which similarly seeks to project models of behaviour to imitate and thus knit subsequent generations into the social fabric.

Although the subjects of the biographies examined in this book were and are important, their biographers have not themselves become well-known, even to specialists of the period. Despite a notable measure of success in social and or economic terms — the foreign-born Paschal became resident French ambassador in the Swiss Grisons, and Ramus's impoverished pupil Nancel wound up as personal physician to a princess, the abbess of Fontrevault, Eléonore de Bourbon — the careers of the biographers studied here show rather less evidence of ability to make much impact on the cultural scene. Read retrospectively, their attempts at self-fashioning on the model of their illustrious subjects have a slightly pathetic, or even comical, quality to them. This prompts the question of the extent to which writing a biography was effective in itself as a strategy for self-promotion within the cultural context of late sixteenth- and early seventeenth-century France. By comparison, the figures studied by Stephen Greenblatt in his *Renaissance Self-Fashioning* — More, Tyndale, Wyatt, Spenser, Shakespeare and Marlowe — 'embody [...] a profound mobility' which was, in most cases, both social and economic.[7] Like the French writers considered here, they were 'talented middle-class men [who] moved out of a narrowly circumscribed social sphere and into a realm that brought them in close contact with the powerful and the great'.[8] In his work, Greenblatt explores the shift attested by the literary production of these representatives of the educated middle class (the exception being the aristocratic Wyatt) away from absorption by community, religious faith, or diplomacy and toward the establishment of literary creation as a profession.[9] The production of works of biography, as shown in the present study, seems to have functioned in largely the reverse direction, with the absorption of the biographer into the social and economic orbit of his subject and his failure to establish himself as a serious literary or cultural figure in his own right. Still, the personal failures of these biographers to make a name for themselves need not invalidate the function they ascribed to biography as a means of securing social and career advancement.

Notes to the Conclusion

1. Becker, *Un Humaniste au XVIe siècle*, p. 28.
2. Becker, *Un Humaniste au XVIe siècle*, p. 29.
3. Gundersheimer, *The Life and Works of Louis Le Roy*.
4. Emmanuelle Mortgat-Longuet discusses Binet's important contribution to the early development of a national history of literature in sixteenth-century France. *Clio au Parnasse. Naissance de l'«histoire littéraire» française aux XVIe et XVIIe siècles* (Paris: Champion, 2006), pp. 67–72 and pp. 85–86.
5. For a general discussion of the place of epideictic rhetoric in early modern biography, see for example, Thomas F. Mayer and D. R. Woolf (eds), 'Introduction' in *The Rhetorics of Life-Writing in Early Modern Europe* (Ann Arbor: University of Michigan Press, 1995), pp. 1–37.
6. Adam Sisman, *Boswell's Presumptuous Task* (London: Penguin, 2001), p. xviii.
7. Greenblatt, *Renaissance Self-Fashioning*, p. 7.
8. Ibid.
9. Ibid., p. 8.

BIBLIOGRAPHY

Primary Works

ANON, *Regime de vivre, et conservation du corps humain* (Paris: Vincent Sertenas, 1561)

AUSONIUS, *Decimi magni Ausonii Burdigalensis opuscula*, ed. by Sesto Prete (Leipzig: Teubner, 1978)

BANOS, THÉOPHILE DE, *P. Rami vita*, in Petrus Ramus, *Commentariorum de religione christiana libri quatuor, nunquam antea editi: eiusdem vita, a Theophilo Banosio descripta* (Frankfurt: A. Wechel, 1576)

BACON, FRANCIS, *The Major Works*, edited with an Introduction and Notes by Brian Vickers (Oxford: Oxford University Press, 2002)

BEAUJOYEULX, BALTHAZAR DE, *Le Balet Comique by Balthazar de Beaujoyeulx, 1581.* A Facsimile with an Introduction by Margaret M. McGowan (Binghamton, NY: Center for Medieval & Renaissance Studies, 1982)

BELLEAU, REMY, *Commentaire au second livre des «Amours» de Ronsard*, ed. by M.-M. Fontaine and F. Lecercle (Geneva: Droz, 1986)

BINET, CLAUDE, *Diverses poësies*, in Jean Bastier de La Péruse, *Les Œuvres de J. Bastier de La Péruse* (Paris: Nicolas Bonfons, 1573), fols. 140–78

——*Les plaisirs de la vie rustique qui sont divers poemes sur ce sujet extraits de plusieurs excellens Autheurs de nostre temps* (Paris: veuve Lucas Breyer, 1583)

——*La Vie de P. de Ronsard de Claude Binet (1586).* Edition critique avec introduction et commentaire historique et critique (Paris: Hachette, 1910)

BOISSARD, JEAN-JACQUES, *Icones uirorum illustrium, doctrina et eruditione præstantium..., II. Pars* (Frankfurt: Théodore De Bry, 1592)

BUDÉ, GUILLAUME, *Philologie. De Philologia.* ed. and trans. by M.-M. de la Garanderie (Paris: Les Belles Lettres, 2001)

——*L'Etude des lettres.* ed. and trans. by Marie-Madeleine de la Garanderie (Paris: Les Belles Lettres, 1988)

——*Correspondance. Tome 1. Les Lettres grecques*, traduction, introduction et notes par Guy Lavoie (Sherbrooke, Quebec: Centre d'Etudes de la Renaissance, 1977)

——*De l'institution du Prince* (Paris: Nicole, 1547 ; repr. Farnborough, Hants: Gregg Press, 1966)

——*Opera omnia*, ed. Celio Secondo Curione (Basel: N. Episcopius, 1557; repr. Farnborough, Hants: Gregg Press, 1966)

——*Epistolæ Gulielmi Budæi, Secretarii Regii* (Paris: J. Bade, 1520)

——*Epistolæ Gulielmi Budæi, Secretarii Regii. Posteriores* (Paris: J. Bade, 1522)

——*G. Budæi...epistolarum latinarum lib. V. Annotationibusque adjectis in singulas fere epistolas. Græcarum item lib. I.* (Paris: J. Bade, 1531)

CICERO, *De officiis*, trans. by Walter Miller (London: W. Heinemann; New York: MacMillan, 1913)

——*De inventione. De optimo genere oratorum. Topica*, trans. by H. M. Hubbell (London: Heinemann; Cambridge, MA: Harvard University Press, 1949)

Critton, George, *Laudatio funebris habita in exequiis Petri Ronsardi* (Paris: A. D'Auvel, 1586)
D'Aubigné, Agrippa, *Œuvres complètes*, ed. by Henri Weber, Jacques Bailbé, and Marguerite Soulié (Paris: Gallimard, 1969)
——*Les Tragiques*, ed. by I. D. McFarlane (London: Athlone Press, 1970)
——*Sa Vie à ses enfants*, ed. by Gilbert Schrenck (Paris: Nizet, 1986)
——*Histoire universelle*, ed. by André Thierry, 11 vols (Geneva: Droz, 1981–2000)
——*Les Tragiques*, ed. by Jean-Raymond Fanlo, 2 vols (Paris: Honoré Champion, 1995)
Du Bellay, Joachim, *Deffense et illustration de la langue françoyse*, in *Œuvres complètes*, ed. by Francis Goyet and Olivier Millet, 2 vols (Paris: H. Champion, 2003–), 1
Du Perron, Jacques Davy, *Oraison funebre sur la mort de Monsieur de Ronsard* (Paris: Federic Morel, 1586)
——*Oraison funebre sur la mort de Monsieur de Ronsard*, ed. by Michel Simonin (Geneva: Droz, 1985)
Erasmus, Desiderius, *Opus epistolarum Des. Erasmi Roterdami*, ed. by Percy Stafford Allen, 12 vols (Oxford: Clarendon Press, 1906–58)
Freige, Jean Thomas, *Petri Rami vita*, in Petrus Ramus, *Prælectiones in Ciceronis orationes octo consulares* (Basel: J. Perna, 1575), pp. 5–46
Galen, *De l'utilité qui provient du jeu de paume au corps et à l'esprit*, trans. by Forbet L'Aisné (Paris: T. Sevestre, 1599)
——*On the Therapeutic Method. Books and I and II.* Translated with an introduction and commentary by R. J. Hankinson (Oxford: Clarendon Press, 1991)
——*On My Own Opinions*, ed. by Vivian Nutton (Berlin: Akademie Verlag, 1999)
——*Selected Works*, trans. by P. N. Singer (Oxford: Oxford University Press, 1997)
——*On the Properties of Foodstuffs*, introduction, translation and commentary by Owen Powell (Cambridge: Cambridge University Press, 2003)
Gentili, Alberico, *De legationibus libri tres* (London: Thomas Vautrollier, 1585)
Hippocrates, *Hippocrates* IV, trans. by W. H. S. Jones (London: Heineman, 1931)
La Framboisière, Nicolas-Abraham de, *Gouvernement nécessaire à chacun pour vivre longuement en santé* (Paris: Michel Sonnius, 1601)
La Fresnaye, Jean Vauquelin de, *L'Art poëtique de Vauquelin de la Fresnaye*, ed. by Georges Pellissier (Paris: Garnier, 1885) [reprint of 1605 text]
La Taille, Jean de, *L'Art de la tragédie*, ed. by Frederick West (Manchester: Manchester University Press, 1939)
Le Roy, Louis, *Gulielmi Budæi Vita per Ludovicum Regium, ad Gulielmum Poietum magnum Franciæ cancellarium* (Paris: Jean Roigny, 1540)
——*Le Sympose de Platon, ou de l'Amour et de beauté, traduict de grec en français* (Paris: Vincent Sertenas, 1559)
——*Consideration sur l'histoire francoise et l'universelle de ce Temps, dont les merveilles sont succinctement recitees* (Paris: Federic Morel, 1579)
——*De la vicissitude ou variete des choses en l'univers, et concurrence des armes et des lettres par les premieres et plus illustres nations du monde, depuis le temps où a commencé la civilité, et memoire humaine jusques à present* (Paris: Pierre L'Huilier, 1576)
L'Estoile, Pierre de, *Registre-Journal du règne de Henri III*, ed. by Madeleine Lazard and Gilbert Schrenck, 6 vols (Geneva: Droz, 1992–2006)
Maggi, Ottaviano, *De legato libri duo* (Venice: [Ludovico Avanzi?], 1566)
Malaspina, Torquato, *Dello scrivere le vite*, ed. by Vanni Bramanti (Bergamo: Moretti & Vitali, 1991)
Marguerite de Valois, *Mémoires et autres écrits: 1574–1614*, édition critique par Eliane Viennot (Paris: Champion, 1999)
Montaigne, Michel de, *Les Essais*, ed. by Pierre Villey, 3rd corrected edn, 3 vols (Paris: Presses universitaires françaises, 1999) [First edn, 1965]

Muret, Marc-Antoine de, *Commentaires au premier livre des «Amours» de Ronsard*, ed. by J. Chomarat, M.-M. Fragonard and G. Mathieu Castellani (Geneva: Droz, 1985)

Nancel, Nicolas, *Analogia microcosmi ad macrocosmon* (Paris: C. Morel, 1611)

—— *Catalogus librorum ab auctore scriptorum* (Paris: Claude Morel, 1603), in Sharratt (2004)

—— *Petri Rami Vita*, in *Declamationum liber eas complectens orationes, quas vel ipse juvenis habuit ad populum, vel per discipulos recitavit, tum Lutetiæ olim docens, tum in Academia duacensi regius professor institutus, in quibus præcipua est medicinæ... apologia et jurisprudentiæ encomium* (Paris: Claude Morel, 1600 [1599])

—— *De legitimo partus tempore* (Paris: J. Richerium, 1586)

—— *Discours de la Peste* (Paris: Denys Du Val, 1581)

Paschalius, Carolus, *C. Cornelii Taciti ... ab excessu Divi Augusti Annalium libri quatuor priores, et in hos observationes C. Paschalii* (Paris: Robert Colombel, 1581)

—— *Vidi Fabricii Pibrachii Vita, scriptore Carolo Paschalio...* (Paris: Robert Colombel, 1584)

—— *Coronæ, opus decem librum distinctum* (Paris: A. Perier, 1610)

—— *Legatus. Opus Caroli Paschalii Regis in Sacro Consistorio Consiliarii et Apud Rhætos Legati. Altera editio non paucis locupletata* (Paris: P. Chevalier, 1612)

—— *Legatio rhetica, sive relatio earum qui interdecennium in Rhætia acciderunt ab anno 1602 ad annum 1614* (Paris: P. Chevalier, 1620)

—— *La Vie et mœurs de messire Guy du Faur, seigneur de Pybrac ... faite par messire Charles Paschal, ... Traduicte du Latin, par Guy du Faur, seigneur de Hermay* (Paris: Thibault du Val, 1617)

—— *La Vie et mœurs de messire Guy du Faur, seigneur de Pybrac ...*, in *Archives curieuses de l'histoire de France*, ed. by Cimber and Danjou, 1st series, 15 vols (Paris: Beauvais, 1834–37), x (1836), pp. 219–97

Petrarca, Francesco, *Canzoniere. Rerum vulgarium fragmenta*, ed. by Rosanna Bettarini, 2 vols (Turin: Einaudi, 2005)

Pibrac, Guy du Faur de, *Ornatissimi cuiusdam viri de rebus Gallicis ad Stanislaum Elvidium epistola* (Paris: Frédéric Morel, 1573)

—— *Les Plaisirs de la vie rustique* (Paris: Federic Morel, 1574 [1575])

—— *Un essai de propagande française à l'étranger. L'Apologie de la Saint-Barthélemy*, ed. and trans. by Alain Cabos (Paris: Champion & Cocharaux, 1922)

—— *Les Quatrains. Les Plaisirs de la vie rustique et autres poésies*, Textes édités, introduits et commentés par Loris Petris (Geneva: Droz, 2004)

Plutarch, *The Rise and Fall of Athens*, trans. by Ian Scott-Kilvert (Harmondsworth: Penguin, 1960)

—— *The Age of Alexander*, trans. by Ian Scott-Kilvert (Harmondsworth: Penguin, 1973)

Porta, Giovan Battista della, *De humana physiognomonia* (Vico Equense: Giuseppe Cacchi, 1586; repr. Naples: Tarquinio Longo, 1602)

—— *Della Fisionomia dell'huomo ... libri sei ... tradotto da latino in volgare* (Naples: G. G. Carlino & C. Vitale, 1610; repr. Vicenza: P. Tozzi, 1615)

Ramée, Pierre de la, *Arguments in Rhetoric against Quintilian: Translation and Text of Peter Ramus's 'Rhetoricæ Distinctiones in Quintilianum' (1549)*, trans. by Carole Newlands, intro. by James Murphy (DeKalb, IL: Northern Illinois Press, 1986)

Rocca, Bartolomeo della, *Le Compendion et brief enseignement de physiognomie et chiromancie* (Paris: P. Drouart, 1546)

Ronsard, Pierre de, *Œuvres complètes*, ed. by Jean Céard, Daniel Ménager, and Michel Simonin, 2 vols (Paris: Gallimard, 1993)

Sainte-Marthe, Scévole de, *Virorum doctrina illustrium, qui hoc seculo in Gallia floruerunt, Elogia* (Poitiers: J. Blanchet, 1598)

Sommi, Leone de', *Quattro dialoghi in materia di rappresentazione sceniche*, ed. by Ferruccio Marotti (Milan: Edizioni Il Polifilo, 1968)

Velliard, Jacques, *Petri Ronsard, poetæ gallici laudatio funebris* (Paris: Denis Du Pré, 1586)
Vera y Figueroa, Juan Antonio de, *Le parfait ambassadeur*, trans. by Nicolas Lancelot (Paris: A. de Sommaville, 1635; repr. [Amsterdam?]: [n. publ.], 1642)

Secondary Works

Andersson, Benedikte, 'Du code autobiographique à la lecture biographique: Claude Binet, lecteur de Ronsard', in *Problématiques de l'autobiographie*, Littérales, 33 (Paris: Centre des Sciences de la Littérature Française, 2004), pp. 33–38
Anderson, Judith H., *Biographical Truth: The Representation of Historical Persons in Tudor–Stuart Writing* (New Haven, CT: Yale University Press, 1984)
Bailbé, Jacques, *Agrippa d'Aubigné, poète des Tragiques* (Caen: Association des publications de la faculté des Lettres et Sciences humaines, 1968)
Barolsky, Paul, *Michelangelo's Nose: A Myth and its Maker* (University Park: Pennsylvania State University Press, 1990)
Becker, Abraham Henri, *Un Humaniste au XVIe siècle. Loys Le Roy (Ludovicus Regius) de Coutances* (Paris: Oudin, 1896)
Bell, David A., *Lawyers and Citizens: The Making of a Political Elite in Old Regime France* (New York: Oxford University Press, 1994)
Biagioli, Mario, *Galileo Courtier: The Practice of Science in the Culture of Absolutism* (Chicago: University of Chicago Press, 1993)
Blunt, Anthony, *Philibert de l'Orme* (London: A. Zwemmer, 1958)
Boucher, Jacqueline, *La Cour de Henri III* (Rennes: Ouest-France, 1986)
Bouwsma, William J., *The Waning of the Renaissance, 1550–1640* (New Haven, CT: Yale University Press, 2000)
Brockliss, Lawrence, and Jones, Colin, *The Medical World of Early Modern France* (Oxford: Clarendon Press, 1997)
Brody, Jules, *Lectures de Montaigne* (Lexington, KY: French Forum, 1982)
Burke, Peter, *What is Cultural History?* (Cambridge: Polity Press, 2004)
——'A Invenção da Biografia e o Individualismo Renascentista', *Estudos Históricos, Rio de Janeiro*, 19 (1997), 1–14
——*The Fortunes of the Courtier* (University Park: Pennsylvania State University Press, 1996)
——'The Renaissance, Individualism and the Portrait', *History of European Ideas*, 21 (1995), 393–400
——'Tacitism', in *Tacitus*, ed. by T. A. Dorey (London: Routledge & Kegan Paul, 1969), pp. 149–71
Cabos, Alain, *Guy du Faur de Pibrac, un magistrat poète au seizième siècle* (Paris: Champion & Cocharaux, 1922)
Cardon, Georges, *La Fondation de l'université de Douai* (Paris: Alcan, 1892)
Céard, Jean, 'La Culture du corps: Montaigne et la diététique de son temps', in *Le Parcours des Essais. Montaigne 1588–1988*, ed. by Marcel Tetel and G. Mallory Masters (Paris: Aux Amateurs de livres, 1989), pp. 83–96
——'La Diététique dans la médicine de la Renaissance', in *Pratiques et discours alimentaires à la Renaissance*, ed. by J. C. Margolin and R. Sauzet (Paris: Maissonneuve et Larose, 1982) pp. 20–36
Chomarat, Jacques, *Prosateurs latins en France au XVIe siècle* (Paris: Presses de la Sorbonne, 1987)
Claretie, Jules, 'Notice', in Guy du Faur de Pibrac, *Les Quatrains. Suivis de ses autres poésies* (Paris: A. Lemerre, 1874; repr. Geneva: Slatkine Reprints, 1969)
Cochrane, Eric, *Historians and Historiography in the Italian Renaissance* (Chicago: University of Chicago Press, 1981)

COTTRELL, ROBERT, *Brantôme, the Writer as Portraitist of his Age* (Geneva: Droz, 1970)

COUZINET, MARIE-DOMINIQUE and MANDOSIO, JEAN-MARC, 'Nouveaux éclairages sur les cours de Ramus et de ses collègues au collège de Presles d'après des notes inédites prises par Nancel', in *Ramus et l'Université* (Paris: Presses de l'ENS, 2004), pp. 11–48

D'AMAT, ROMAN, *Dictionnaire de biographie française*, fasc. 80 (Paris: Letouzey & Ané, 1929–)

DASSONVILLE, MICHEL. *Ronsard. Etude historique et littéraire*, 5 vols (Geneva: Droz, 1968–90)

DESAN, PHILIPPE, *Penser l'histoire à la renaissance* (Caen: Paradigme, 1993)

DAVIES, KATHARINE, 'Leonardo Porzio in the 1527 *De asse*', in *Acta Conventus Neo-Latini Bononiensis*, ed. by Richard J. Schoeck (Binghampton, NY: Center for Medieval and Renaissance Studies, 1985), pp. 430–36

DICKENS, A. G., *The Counter-Reformation* (London: Thames & Hudson, 1968)

DUBOIS, CLAUDE-GILBERT, 'L'Individu dans la société et dans l'histoire. Formes de la biographie dans la période 1560–1600', *Nouvelle Revue du Seizième Siècle*, 19.1 (2001), 83–105

DUPÈBE, JEAN, 'Un chancelier humaniste sous François Ier: François Olivier (1497–1560)', in *Humanism and Letters in the Age of François Ier*, ed. by Philip Ford and Gillian Jondorf (Cambridge: Cambridge French Colloquia, 1996), pp. 87–114

EICHEL-LOJKINE, PATRICIA, *Le Siècle des grands hommes. Les Recueils de vies d'hommes illustres au XVIème siècle* (Louvain and Sterling, VA: Peeters, 2001)

EVANS, E. C., 'Roman Descriptions of Personal Appearance in History and Biography', *Harvard Studies in Classical Philology*, 46 (1935), 43–84

FAISANT, CLAUDE, *Mort et Résurrection de la Pléiade*, ed. J. Rieu (Paris: Champion, 1998)

FANTONI, CHRISTIAN, 'Henri IV burlesque dans *Les avantures du Baron de Fœneste* d'Agrippa d'Aubigné', *Nouvelle revue du XVIe siècle*, 19.2 (2001), 69–81

FRENCH, R. K., 'The Medical Ethics of Gabriele de Zerbi', in *Doctors and Ethics: The Earlier Historical Setting of Professional Ethics*, ed. by Andrew Wear, Joanna Geyer-Kordesch and R. K. French (Amsterdam: Rodopi, 1993) pp. 72–97

FUMAROLI, MARC, *L'Age de l'éloquence. Rhétorique et «res literaria» au seuil de l'époque classique* (Geneva: Droz, 1980)

——'Les Mémoires au XVIIe siècle au carrefour des genres', *XVIIe siècle*, 94/95 (1971), 7–37

GADOFFRE, GILBERT, *La Révolution culturelle dans la France des humanistes. Guillaume Budé et François Ier* (Geneva: Droz, 1997)

GARCÍA BALLESTER, LUIS, 'Soul and Body: Disease of the Soul and Disease of the Body in Galen's Medical Thought', in *Galen and Galenism: Theory and Medical Practice from Antiquity to the European Renaissance*, ed. by Jon Arrizabalaga, Montserrat Cabré, Lluís Cifuentes, and Fernando Salmón (Aldershot: Ashgate, 2002), pp. 117–52

——'On the origin of the "six non-natural things" in Galen', *Galen und das hellenistische Erbe. Verhandlungen des IV. Internationalen Galen-Symposiums*, ed. by J. Kollesch and D. Nickel (Stuttgart: Franz Steiner, 1993), pp. 105–15

GILROY, JAMES P., 'The Theme of "Etre" and "Paraître" in the Works of Agrippa d'Aubigné', *The Bulletin of the Rocky Mountain Modern Language Association*, 27 (1973), 205–11

GORDON, ALEX, *Ronsard et la rhétorique* (Geneva: Droz, 1970)

GRANT, MARK, *Galen on Food and Diet* (London: Routledge, 2000)

GREENBERG, MITCHELL, 'Baroque History: Style and Structure in the "Histoire Universelle"' (unpublished doctoral dissertation, University of California at Berkeley, 1973; abstract in *Dissertation abstracts*, 27.9, 5815-A)

GREENBLATT, STEPHEN, *Sir Walter Ralegh: The Renaissance Man and his Roles* (New Haven, CT: Yale University Press, 1973)

——*Renaissance Self-Fashioning* (Chicago: University of Chicago Press, 1980)

Greene, Thomas M., *The Light in Troy: Imitation and Discovery in Renaissance Poetry* (New Haven, CT: Yale University Press, 1982)

Groebner, Valentin, 'Inside Out: Clothes, Dissimulation, and the Arts of Accounting in the Autobiography of Matthaus Schwarz, 1496–1574', *Representations*, 66 (1999), 100–21

Gundersheimer, Werner L., *The Life and Works of Louis Le Roy* (Geneva: Droz, 1966)

Hampton, Timothy, *Writing from History: The Rhetoric of Exemplarity in Renaissance Literature* (Ithaca, NY: Cornell University Press, 1990)

Hooykaas, Reijer, 'Pierre de la Ramée et l'empirisme scientifique au XVIe siècle', in *La Science au seizième siècle. Colloque international Royaumont, 1–4 juillet 1957* (Paris: Hermann, 1960), pp. 297–311

Huppert, George, *Les Bourgeois Gentilshommes: An Essay on the Definition of Elites in Renaissance France* (Chicago: The University of Chicago Press, 1977)

Ijsewijn, Jozef, 'Humanistic Autobiography', in *Studia Humanitatis. Ernesto Grassi zum 70. Geburtstag*, ed. by E. Hora and E. Kessler (Munich: W. Fink, 1973), pp. 209–17

——'Die humanistische Biographie', in *Biographie und Autobiographie in der Renaissance. Arbeitsgespräch in der Herzog August Bibliothek Wolfenbüttel vom 1. bis 3. November 1982*, ed. August Buck (Wiesbaden: O. Harrassowitz, 1983), pp. 1–19

Jardine, Lisa, *Erasmus, Man of Letters: The Construction of Charisma in Print* (Princeton, NJ: Princeton University Press, 1993)

Jones, Ann Rosalind and Stallybrass, Peter, 'The Circulation of Clothes and the Making of the English Theatre', in *Renaissance Clothing and the Materials of Memory* (Cambridge: Cambridge University Press, 2000), pp. 175–206

Katz, R. A., *Ronsard's French Critics, 1585–1828* (Geneva: Droz, 1966)

Kelley, Donald, *Foundations of Modern Historical Scholarship: Language, Law and History in the French Renaissance* (New York: Columbia University Press, 1970)

Kennedy, George A., *Classical Rhetoric and its Christian and Secular Tradition from Ancient to Modern Times* (London: Croon Helm, 1980)

Knecht, Robert J., *Catherine de' Medici* (London: Longman, 1998)

Knös, Börje, *Un ambassadeur de l'hellénisme. Janus Lascaris et la tradition gréco-byzantine dans l'humanisme français* (Uppsala and Stockholm: Almqvist & Wiksells, 1945)

Kuperty-Tsur, Nadine, 'Aspects de la rhétorique d'Agrippa d'Aubigné dans *Sa Vie à ses enfants*', *Albineana*, 13 (2001), 105–18

Lafond, Jean, *Moralistes du XVIIe siècle* (Paris: R. Laffont, 1992)

La Garanderie, M.-M., 'Guillaume Budé, a Philosopher of Culture', *The Sixteenth Century Journal*, 19 (1988), 379–87

——*Christianisme & lettres profanes. Essai sur l'Humanisme français (1515–1535) et sur la pensée de Guillaume Budé* (Paris: H. Champion, 1995)

Langer, Ullrich, *Invention, Death and Self-Definitions in the Poetry of Ronsard* (Saratoga, CA: ANMA Libri, 1986)

——'Poétique de la *responce* dans *Sa vie à ses enfants*', in *Poétiques d'Aubigné: Actes du colloque de Genève* (Geneva: Droz, 1996), pp. 207–16

——*Vertu du Discours, Discours de la Vertu. Littérature et philosophie morale au XVIe siècle en France* (Geneva: Droz, 1999)

Lavoie, Guy, 'G. Budé à son médecin. Un inédit sur sa maladie', *Renaissance and Reformation/ Renaissance et Réforme*, n.s. 15.1 (1991), 37–56

Laumonier, Paul, 'Introduction', in *La Vie de P. de Ronsard de Claude Binet (1586).* Edition critique avec introduction et commentaire historique et critique (Paris: Hachette, 1910)

——'La Cassandre de Ronsard', *Revue de la Renaissance*, 1902

Lecercle, François, *La Chimère de Zeuxis. Portrait poétique et portrait peint en France et Italie à la Renaissance*, Etudes littéraires françaises, 26 (Tübingen: Gunter Narr Verlag, 1987)

Lejeune, Philippe, *L'Autobiographie en France* (Paris: A. Colin, 1971)

——*Le Pacte autobiographique* (Paris: Seuil, 1975)

Le Person, Xavier, *'Practiques' et 'Practiqueurs': La Vie politique à la fin du règne de Henri III (1584–1589)* (Geneva: Droz, 2002)

Linden, David E. J., 'Gabriele de Zerbi's *De cautelis medicorum* and the Tradition of Medical Prudence', *Bulletin of the History of Medicine*, 73 (1999), 19–37

Lyons, John, *Exemplum: The Rhetoric of Example in Early Modern France and Italy* (Princeton, NJ: Princeton University Press, 1989)

Maclean, Ian, *Logic, Signs and Nature in the Renaissance: The Case of Learned Medicine* (Cambridge: Cambridge University Press, 2002)

Magnien, Michel, 'Portrait de Budé en "intellectuel". La *G. Budœi viri clarissimi vita* de Loys Le Roy (1540)', *Renaissance and Reformation* 24.4 (2000), 29–48

——and Meerhoff, Kees (eds.), *Ramus et l'université* (Paris: Editions rue d'Ulm, 2004)

Martinet, Jean-Luc, 'L'Excellence de l'homme dans le livre *De la vicissitude ou variété des choses en l'univers* de Louis Le Roy', in *Histoire et littérature au siècle de Montaigne. Mélanges offertes à Claude-Gilbert Dubois*, ed. by Françoise Argod-Dutard, Cahiers d'Humanisme et Renaissance, 60 (Geneva: Droz, 2001), pp. 301–12

Mattingly, Garrett, *Renaissance Diplomacy* (London: Cape, 1955)

Mayer, Thomas F. and Woolf, D. R. (eds.), *The Rhetorics of Life-Writing in Early Modern Europe* (Ann Arbor: University of Michigan Press, 1995)

McGowan, Margaret M., *Le Balet comique by Balthazar de Beaujoyeulx, 1581*, a facsimile with an introduction by Margaret M. McGowan (Binghampton, NY: Center for Medieval and Renaissance Studies, 1982)

McLaughlin, Martin L., *Literary Imitation in the Renaissance: The Theory and Practice of Literary Imitation in Italy from Dante to Bembo* (Oxford: Clarendon Press, 1995)

McNeil, David O., *Guillaume Budé and Humanism in the Reign of Francis I* (Geneva: Droz, 1975)

McVaugh, Michael R., 'Bedside Manners in the Middle Ages', *Bulletin of the History of Medicine*, 71 (1997), 201–23

Meerhoff, Kees, *Rhétorique et poétique au XVIe siècle en France. Du Bellay, Ramus et les autres* (Leiden: E. J. Brill, 1986)

Ménager, Daniel, *Ronsard. Le Roi, le Poète et les Hommes* (Geneva: Droz, 1979)

——'Théodore de Bèze, Biographe de Calvin', *Bibliothèque d'Humanisme et Renaissance*, 45 (1983), 231–55

——*Diplomatie et théologie à la Renaissance* (Paris: Presses universitaires françaises, 2001)

Michaud, Joseph L. and Michaud, Louis Gabriel, *Biographie universelle ancienne et moderne*, 45 vols (Paris: Desplaces, 1854–65)

Momigliano, Arnaldo, 'The First Political Commentary on Tacitus', in *Contributo alla storia degli studi classici*, Storia e letteratura. Raccolta di studi e testi, 47 (Rome: Edizioni di Storia e Letteratura, 1955), pp. 37–59

——'Tacitus and the Tacitean Tradition', in *The Classical Foundations of Modern Historiography*, foreword by Riccardo Di Donato (Berkeley: University of California Press, 1990), pp. 109–31

Mortgat-Longuet, Emmanuelle, *Clio au Parnasse. Naissance de l'«histoire littéraire» française aux XVIe et XVIIe siècles* (Paris: Champion, 2006)

Moss, Ann, 'Literary Imitation in the Sixteenth Century: Writers and Readers, Latin and French', in *The Cambridge History of Literary Criticism. Volume III. The Renaissance*, ed. by G. P. Norton (Cambridge: Cambridge University Press, 1999), pp. 107–18

Mullett, Michael A., *The Catholic Reformation* (London: Routledge, 1999)

Newton, Stella Mary, *Renaissance Theatre Costume and the Sense of the Historic Past* (London: Rapp & Whiting, 1975)

Nutton, Vivian, 'Galen and Medical Autobiography', *Proceedings of the Cambridge Philological Society*, 198 (1972), 50–62

——*Ancient Medicine* (Abingdon: Routledge, 2004)

O'BRIEN, JOHN, 'At Montaigne's Table', *French Studies*, 54.1 (2000), 1–16

OLDRINI, GUIDO, 'Eduquer au savoir. La Formation ramiste entre Université et société', in *Ramus et l'université* (Paris: Editions rue d'Ulm, 2004), pp. 173–88

OMONT, HENRI, *Georges Hermonyme de Sparte, maître de grec à Paris et copiste de manuscrits suivi d'une notice sur les collections de manuscrits de Jean et Guillaume Budé et de notes sur leur famille*, extrait des *Mémoires* et du *Bulletin de la Société de l'histoire de Paris et de l'Ile de France*, 12 (Paris: Nogent-le-Rotrou, 1885)

ONG, WALTER J., *Ramus: Method, and the Decay of Dialogue: From the Art of Discourse to the Art of Reason* (Cambridge, MA: Harvard University Press, 1958)

PASK, KEVIN, *The Emergence of the English Author: Pre-Scripting the Life of the Poet in Early Modern England* (Cambridge: Cambridge University Press, 1996)

PERCEAU, LOUIS and THIBAULT, GENEVIÈVE, *Bibliographie des poésies de P. de Ronsard mises en musique au XVIe siècle* (Paris: Droz, 1941)

PÉROUSE DE MONTCLOS, JEAN-MARIE, *Philibert de l'Orme. Architecte du roi (1514–1570)* (Paris: Mengès, 2000)

PERSAN, MARQUIS DE, *Une mission diplomatique en Pologne au XVIe siècle. Jacques Faye d'Espeisses et Guy du Faur de Pibrac. 1574–1575. D'après certains documents inédits. Extrait de la Revue d'histoire diplomatique* (Paris: Plon-Nourrit, 1904)

PINVERT, LUCIEN, *Lazare de Baïf (1496?–1547)* (Paris: A. Fontemoing, 1900)

PLATTARD, JEAN, *Agrippa d'Aubigné. Une figure de premier plan dans nos Lettres de la Renaissance* (Paris: Boivin, 1931)

PORÉE, CHARLES, *Un parlementaire sous François Ier: Guillaume Poyet (1473–1548)* (Angers: Germain et G. Grassin, 1898)

POSNER, DAVID MATTHEW, *The Performance of Nobility in Early Modern European Literature* (Cambridge: Cambridge University Press, 1999)

QUAINTON, MALCOLM, 'The Liminary Texts of Ronsard's *Amours de Cassandre* (1552): Poetics, Erotics, Semiotics', *French Studies*, 53.3 (1999), 257–78

RANDALL COATS, CATHERINE, 'Representing and Re-Presenting the Self: Fact and Fiction in Agrippa d'Aubigné's "Sa Vie à ses enfants" and the "Histoire universelle"', *South Atlantic Review*, 54.2 (May 1989) 23–40

——'A Protestant Poetics of Process: Reformation Rhetorics of the Self in Sponde, de Bèze and d'Aubigné', in *The Rhetorics of Life-Writing in Early Modern Europe*, ed. by Thomas F. Mayer and D. R. Woolf (Ann Arbor: University of Michigan Press, 1995), pp. 223–42

REGOSIN, RICHARD, 'D'Aubigné's *Les Tragiques*: Divine Tragedy', *Bibliothèque d'Humanisme et Renaissance*, 28 (1966), 52–73

RICHTER, BODO L. O., 'The Thought of Louis Le Roy According to his Early Pamphlets', *Studies in the Renaissance*, 8 (1961), 173–96

ROCHE, DANIEL, *La Culture des apparances. Une histoire du vêtement. XVIIe — XVIIIe siècle* (Paris: Fayard, 1989)

SANDY, GERALD, 'Guillaume Budé: Philologist and Polymath: A Preliminary Study', in *The Classical Heritage in France* (Leiden: Brill, 2002), pp. 79–108

SCHRENCK, GILBERT, 'A. d'Aubigné, *Sa Vie à ses enfants*. Approches et mises en perspective', *Réforme Humanisme Renaissance*, 10 (1979), 3–11

——'Aspects de l'écriture autobiographique au XVIe siècle: A. d'Aubigné et *Sa Vie à ses enfants*', *Nouvelle Revue du Seizième Siècle*, 3 (1985), 33–51

——'Introduction', in Agrippa d'Aubigné, *Sa Vie à ses enfants*, ed. by Gilbert Schrenck (Paris: Nizet, 1986), pp. 11–36

SHARRATT, PETER, 'Nicolaus Nancelius, *Petri Rami Vita*, edited with an English translation', *Humanistica Lovaniensia*, 24 (1975), 161–277

——'Nicolas de Nancel (1539–1610)', in *Acta Conventus Neo-Latini Amsteldamensis* (Munich: Wilhelm Fink Verlag, 1979), pp. 918–27

——'Nicolas de Nancel: A Medical and Theological View of the Other Sex', in *Female Saints and Sinners: Saintes et Mondaines (France 1450–1650)*, ed. by Jennifer Britnell and Ann Moss (Durham: University of Durham, 2002), pp. 109–21

——'The Lost Library of Nicolas de Nancel', *History of Universities*, 19.2 (2004), 1–90

SIMAR, THÉOPHILE, *Christophe de Longueil, Humaniste* (Louvain: Bureaux du Recueil, 1911)

SIRAISI, NANCY G., *Medieval and Early Renaissance Medicine: An Introduction to Knowledge and Practice* (Chicago: University of Chicago Press, 1990)

——'Medicine, Physiology and Anatomy in Early Sixteenth-Century Critiques of the Arts and the Sciences,' in *New Perspectives on Renaissance Thought: Essays in the History of Science, Education and Philosophy in Memory of Charles B. Schmitt*, ed. by John Henry and Sarah Hutton (London: Duckworth, 1990), pp. 214–19.

——*The Clock and the Mirror: Girolamo Cardano and Renaissance Medicine* (Princeton, NJ: Princeton University Press, 1997)

SISMAN, ADAM, *Boswell's Presumptuous Task* (London: Penguin, 2001)

SKALNIK, JAMES VEAZIE, *Ramus and Reform: University and Church at the End of the Renaissance*, Sixteenth Century essays and studies, 60 (Kirksville, MO: Truman State University Press, 2002)

SMITH, PAUL J., 'Rabelais' *Pantagruel* and *Gargantua* as Mock-Biographies', in *Modelling the Individual: Biography and Portrait in the Renaissance*, ed. by Karl Enenkel, Betsy de Jong-Crane, and Peter Liebregts (Amsterdam and Atlanta, GA: Rodopi, 1998), pp. 153–72

TIERSOT, JULES, *Ronsard et la musique de son temps* (Leipzig: Breitkopf und Haertel, 1903)

URNESS, CAROL, 'Introduction', in François Deserps, *The Various Styles of Clothing*, A Facsimile of the 1562 Edition, ed. by Sara Shannon (Minneapolis: University of Minnesota Press, 2001)

VERDONK, J. J., *Petrus Ramus en de Wiskunde* (Assen: Van Gorcum, 1966)

VIALA, ALAIN, *Naissance de l'écrivain* (Paris: Les Editions de minuit, 1985)

WEAR, A., FRENCH, R. K. and LONIE, I. M. (eds.), *The Medical Renaissance of the Sixteenth Century* (Cambridge: Cambridge University Press, 1985)

WOODALL, JOANNA, 'Introduction: Facing the Subject', in *Portraiture: Facing the Subject*, ed. and intro. by Joanna Woodall (Manchester: Manchester University Press, 1997), pp. 1–28

YATES, FRANCES A., *The Valois Tapestries*, 2nd edn (London: Routledge & Kegan Paul, 1975)

——*The Art of Memory* (Chicago: Chicago University Press, 1966)

ZEMON DAVIS, NATALIE, 'Boundaries and the Sense of Self in Sixteenth-Century France', in *Reconstructing Individualism: Autonomy, Individuality, and the Self in Western Thought*, ed. by Thomas C. Heller, Morton Sosna, and David E. Wellerby, with Arnold I. Davidson, Ann Swidler, and Ian Watt (Stanford, CA: Stanford University Press, 1986), pp. 53–63

INDEX